UNDER A CANOPY OF GRAPES

MICHAEL RUCKER

Copyright © 2026 by Michael Rucker
All rights reserved.

No part of this publication may be reproduced, distributed, or transmitted in any form or by any means, including photocopying, recording, or other electronic or mechanical methods, without the prior written permission of the publisher, except as permitted by U.S. copyright law.

Paperback: 979-8-9949359-0-3
Hardcover: 979-8-9949359-1-0
Ebook: 979-8-9949359-2-7
Book Design by Nuno Moreira, NMDESIGN

UNDER A CANOPY OF GRAPES

Letting Go and Coming Home on the Camino de Santiago

MICHAEL RUCKER

AUTHOR'S NOTE

This memoir reflects the author's recollections of experiences over time. Some events and dialogue have been recreated from memory and, in some cases, compressed or reordered for narrative clarity. To protect the privacy of individuals, some names have been changed.

Dedicated to my mother, Alice, without whom I could not have experienced any of God's graces along the way.

PROLOGUE: THE BENCH

I was still hiding my smoking on the Camino.

Whenever the craving hit, I'd scan ahead for a side street or alley where I could slip away unnoticed. Light up quick. Take a few drags. Stub it out and return to the path like nothing had happened. The shame was worse than the smoking itself—this feeling that I was doing something wrong, that the other pilgrims would judge me, that I wasn't spiritual enough or healthy enough or worthy enough to be walking this sacred route if I couldn't even quit cigarettes.

So, I hid.

That afternoon—September 25, 2022—somewhere between Burgos and León, I found a dead-end street.

It was a beautiful fall day. Blue sky stretched overhead, puffy white clouds drifting across it like they'd been painted there. The air was warm but not hot; that perfect temperature was where you could walk for miles without thinking about the weather. I'd been on the Camino for three weeks by then. Long enough that my body knew the rhythm. Long enough that the themes had started coming—forgiveness, self-compassion, letting go. Long enough that I'd stopped running from myself and started actually looking.

For the past couple of weeks, I'd walked through the Meseta. Those endless fields where there's nowhere to hide from yourself. No shade. No distraction. Just you and the path and whatever you've been carrying. The landscape had stripped me bare, forced me to face things I'd spent decades avoiding. By the time I reached the outskirts of León, I felt hollowed out in a way that was both exhausting and clarifying.

A few hours later, I found a dead-end street.

It sloped downward, narrow and cobblestoned, lined with old stone buildings that looked like they'd been standing there for centuries. No one was around. Just me and the sound of my trail runners on the stone and the cigarette pack in my pocket calling me.

At the end of the street: a bench.

And beyond it, a valley.

I stopped walking and just stood there a moment, looking.

The valley spread out below me—rolling hills covered in sparse brush, red dirt visible between the scrub, wide open space that went on forever. It looked exactly like Globe, Arizona, a little copper-mining town about ninety miles east of Phoenix. Exactly like the landscape where I grew up. The same barren beauty. The same emptiness that somehow felt full.

I put my backpack down. The weight of it lifting off my shoulders felt like relief. I pulled out my cigarettes, lit one, and sat.

The bench was wood. Weathered. Smooth from years of people sitting exactly where I was sitting, looking at exactly what I was looking at.

I took a drag and exhaled slowly, watching the smoke drift away on the breeze.

And something in me settled.

I thought about the steps I'd taken over the last three weeks. Processing childhood trauma and failed relationships and thirty years of drinking to numb the pain. I'd forgiven myself for things I didn't think I could forgive. I'd cried on mountainsides and laughed with strangers and walked so many miles that my body moved without thinking. I'd covered so much ground, literally and emotionally, that I barely recognized the person I'd been when I started.

But sitting on that bench, looking out at that valley, I felt something I hadn't felt in years.

For the first time, I knew who I was.

I was no longer the drunk, scared kid from Globe. Nor was I the man trying to prove he was worthy of love. Nor the brand builder chasing James's promise or Robert's validation.

Just me, Michael, sixty years old, almost one year sober, walking across Spain with a cigarette in his hand and a backpack full of everything he'd been carrying for too long.

Even being a smoker was okay.

I wasn't proud of it. I wasn't pretending it was healthy or spiritual or good. But in that moment, sitting on that bench, it was just part of who I was. And I was okay, proud, and even resolved but not cocky.

I took another drag and let the silence settle around me.

And then I said aloud something I'd never heard myself say.

"I will move onward and forward in the grace of God."

The words came from somewhere deep. I don't know where. But they felt true. They felt like something I'd been trying to say my whole life and finally had the language for.

I paused and let them sit in the air between me and the valley.

And then I said them again.

"I will move onward and forward in the grace of God."

This time, they landed differently, heavier and more real.

I sat there with them, feeling the weight of what I'd just spoken into existence. Talk about a spiritual moment.

A few minutes later, I heard footsteps behind me.

I turned. A woman—another pilgrim—was walking down the dead-end street. She had a backpack, walking poles, the same tired but determined look we all had by that point in the journey.

She saw the bench, and saw me. Then she saw the valley spread out beyond us.

And something in her face changed.

She stopped a few feet away, just looking out at the view. Then she turned to me and smiled.

"Isn't this one of the best kept secrets on the Camino?" she said.

"And you found it."

It wasn't a question, it was more like recognition. She saw the moment I was having and understood the sacredness of it. And she wasn't going to intrude.

But I was so full of this new understanding—so certain of who I was and where I was going—that I couldn't keep it to myself.

"I just said something," I told her. "For the first time. I said: I will move onward and forward in the grace of God."

She looked at me. Really looked at me. And her smile softened.

"Wow," she said quietly. "Thank you for sharing."

She introduced herself. I can't remember her name now. We exchanged pleasantries—where we'd started, where we were headed, how the Camino was treating us. The usual pilgrim conversation.

And then she left.

She walked back up the street and disappeared around the corner, leaving me alone on the bench with my cigarette and my revelation and the valley that looked like home.

I saw her a few more times after that. We'd pass each other on the trail, say hello, keep moving. That's how the Camino works. People come into your life exactly when you need them, bear witness to your moment, and then move on, no attachment, no expectation with just presence.

But she'd been there. She'd heard it. And that's all that mattered.

I sat on that bench a little while longer, finishing my cigarette, looking out at the valley. The sky was still blue. The clouds were still drifting. The hills still looked like Globe.

But something had shifted.

I knew who I was. I knew where I was going. And I knew how I was going to get there.

One step at a time. Onward and forward. In the grace of God.

That was three years ago.

I thought that moment on the bench would be enough. I thought knowing who I was meant I'd figured out how to live. I thought the Camino had saved me, and all I had to do was carry that revelation home and everything would fall into place.

But three years later, I found myself standing in the Pyrenees, preparing to walk again.

Because knowing who you are and learning to stop running are two different things.

The first Camino taught me who I was. The second would teach me something harder.

It would teach me to let go.

PART ONE

THE FIRST CAMINO

CHAPTER ONE: A PILGRIM'S STORY

Where It Begins

Before I ever set foot on the Camino, I had already been walking for most of my life.

Not forward exactly, and not toward anything clearly named, but away from whatever closed my chest and toward whatever felt like air. I learned early that survival did not come from safety but from awareness. From reading a room before it turned. From knowing when to speak and when to disappear. That skill became instinct, and instinct became habit. It carried me through places and people long before I understood what it meant to belong anywhere.

Buster Mounce was the first man who saw me. He did not rescue me. He did not try to fix anything. He simply treated me as if I were already capable. He trusted me with responsibility and spoke to me as if my words mattered. When I made mistakes, he did not rush in with solutions. He stayed still and let me work it out. I always did. Not because I had answers, but because he believed I could find them.

Buster showed me what steady looked like. How to keep your word. How to work without spectacle. How to correct without humiliating. He never told me who to be. He showed me how to stand.

When Buster died, there was no clean ending. His absence arrived quietly, like a door that never opened again. Years later, I learned that they read my letter to him at his funeral. I was not there. I did not know at the time. Somehow that felt right. He had always been a witness. Even in death, he was still holding the story without trying to shape it.

What I learned in foster care was not how to survive on my own. It was that I already had been.

Home had never been safe in the way people mean when they say that word. Safety, for me, was temporary and conditional. Something you sensed rather than trusted. I learned how to stay useful, how to stay alert, how to stay one step ahead of whatever might turn. If I stayed competent, I could usually avoid the worst of it. That way of being followed me into adulthood. It became a strength in business, a liability in intimacy, and a constant hum beneath everything else.

At sixteen I found myself in Bolivia as an exchange student. Bolivia was where the world became real for me.

I arrived young, frightened, eager, and unprepared. The jungle did not care about my history or my fear. It did not soften itself for my comfort. It was vast and alive and loud in a way nothing I had known before had ever been. Life did not hide there. It announced itself constantly.

I loved it.

Bolivia was hard and often unforgiving, but for the first time the world felt open instead of threatening. I wanted to see everything. I wanted to understand how people lived, how joy survived even when circumstances were brutal. It was the first time I felt like I was living the life I was meant to live, not the one I had assembled for safety.

Then adulthood arrived, and with it performance.

I built a career, got married, and learned how to succeed while hiding everything that mattered. When I finally came out, it did not make me whole. It stopped me from dying slowly.

The collapse was thorough. My wife broke her hand the night I left. She called my office every night afterward and left messages saying she was going to kill herself. Her church paid for conversion therapy. Her pastor believed I could be changed. I believed it too, at least enough to try.

At the same time, my gay uncle was dying of AIDS. My brother told me I could not be gay because we were here to procreate. The family asked me to disappear just as the world was punishing people for being seen.

I was not brave. I was exhausted.

What saved me were the people who loved the man underneath the performance. They did not need explanations before they stayed. They loved the person I had been hiding.

Fania came later, and for a long time it looked like proof that everything I had survived meant something.

For more than a decade, we resurrected a label that had defined a culture. We brought it back into the world and made it matter again. Concerts, records, films, and thousands of people dancing together to music that had once been abandoned. It was extraordinary. It was also not mine in the ways that mattered when it ended.

I drank through all of it.

For thirty years, alcohol was constant and rewarded. It helped me sleep. It helped me celebrate. It helped me avoid the parts of myself I did not know how to hold. It did not look like a problem because it fit the life I was living.

By the end, I was drinking two bottles of wine a day, sometimes three. I would wake up and pace the apartment until the shakes subsided enough to pour the first glass. The glass became the morning. The morning became the afternoon. By evening, the edges had softened enough that I could almost believe I was functional.

I was not fooling anyone.

The morning I stopped, there was no dramatic moment, no intervention, no bottom that announced itself clearly. I simply woke up and knew that if I kept drinking, I would die. Not someday but soon.

Alcohol left the room, and when it did, it took with it the insulation I had relied on for decades. Without it, everything felt sharper. Mornings arrived without padding. Memories pressed closer and questions I had postponed for years no longer waited their turn.

When alcohol was gone, something else stepped forward. A deep, quiet depression I had outrun for decades finally caught up with me. Anxiety, long disguised as ambition and productivity, no longer had anywhere to hide. Some days my chest felt tight before I opened my eyes. Other days getting out of bed required negotiation.

Sitting still made it worse.

So I began to walk.

Every morning before sunrise, I stepped into a Miami that felt abandoned. Restaurants were dark, streets were empty. Traffic lights cycled through colors for no one. Without the usual noise and urgency, the city revealed itself quietly, almost tenderly.

At first I walked four miles. Then six. Some mornings it became ten.

One morning I walked to Miami just as the light turned the bay silver. The water was so still it looked like glass, and the sailboats sat motionless at their moorings like they had been painted there. I stopped on a bridge and watched the sky change from black to gray to pale blue, and for the first time in months, I felt my chest open.

It was not happiness. It was not peace. It was just space and room to breathe.

I kept walking.

Some mornings I cried openly at intersections, tears running down my face while traffic lights changed and no one saw. Other mornings I felt nothing at all, just the repetitive motion of my feet and the sound of my breath. Occasionally, without warning, I felt calm.

I moved through neighborhoods I had lived in for years but had never really seen. South of Fifth Street, the beach, over to Brickell and the Design District empty of people, just murals and locked galleries and early light on concrete.

The walks became a ritual, shoes by the door, coffee cooling on the counter and familiar routes slowly expanding. Walking taught my nervous system a different pace. It gave my body a voice my mind could finally hear.

Months later, I realized I had walked nearly a thousand miles.

At the time, I did not know I was training for the Camino. I only knew that walking was keeping me alive. It regulated what alcohol had numbed. It taught me that depression did not mean failure and anxiety did not mean danger. They were signals asking for patience, movement, and care.

When I walked, I could breathe.

I turned sixty and did not know who I was.

When I arrived in Europe, I did not yet know I would walk the Camino. I only knew I was untethered and sober. Tired in a way sleep did not touch, I moved through cities slowly, telling myself I was resting, when what I was really doing was avoiding a decision.

The Camino hovered at the edge of my awareness. Walking meant being alone with myself without anesthesia or distraction. It meant nowhere to hide.

For weeks I circled the same thoughts. I was sixty years old and newly sober and terrified of what I might find if I stopped moving long enough to look. The Camino was five hundred miles long. Five hundred miles of walking with nothing to do but be present with whatever rose up.

I did not know if I was ready.

But I knew I could not go back to Miami without trying. I knew that if I walked away from this, I would spend the rest of my life wondering what I had been too afraid to face.

Two weeks before the start, I decided.

There was no announcement. Just a quiet decision after weeks of circling the same thoughts. I booked what needed to be booked. I packed what little I would carry. I told one friend. Saying it out loud made it real.

I was sixty years old and did not know who I was without the scaffolding I had built around myself. What I did know was that something in me needed to be met honestly.

The road did not promise answers. It only promised movement.

So I chose to walk.

CHAPTER TWO: AFRAID TO START

I landed in London on July 24, 2022, with nine months of sobriety behind me, a carry-on suitcase, a backpack, and no idea what I was doing.

I had closed one chapter of my life without being able to see what came next. Sixty years old, sober, and with no income or plan. Every structure I had built my identity around had collapsed—Fania, the partnerships, the version of myself I had spent decades constructing. I could not go back to that life, but I had no map forward.

I was terrified.

Every trip I had taken to Europe before this one followed the same familiar arc. Four-star hotels. Five-star restaurants. Drinking from the moment the plane landed until I stumbled back to my room at night. I had been to Paris, Barcelona, Rome, London, and Amsterdam, and remembered almost none of it clearly. Just hotel bars and hangovers and the belief that if I kept moving fast enough, I would not have to feel anything.

This time was different because I had no choice. Sobriety had removed the buffer. Everything felt sharper, closer, impossible to avoid.

The Virgin Atlantic flight from Los Angeles took eleven hours, and I spent most of it listening to Brené Brown's *Atlas of the Heart*, a book devoted to naming and understanding human emotions. When I was a child, my stepfather had tried to beat feelings out of me. Later, alcohol numbed whatever survived.

It was disorienting and often unbearable. Emotions arrived without warning—grief, anxiety, shame, hope—and I did not know what to do with them. I did not know how to sit with them or let them move through me. More than once, it made me want to disappear.

Brown's voice in my headphones made it feel possible. She gave language to feelings I had spent a lifetime avoiding, and with language came permission. I would listen to that book three times over the next three months, trying to learn what I should have learned decades earlier.

Learning to Walk Again

I do not remember the exact neighborhood in London where I stayed, only that it was near a large train station and close enough to everything I needed. The Airbnb was small and unremarkable. I walked everywhere. I never took a taxi or the Underground. I walked eight, ten, sometimes twelve miles a day, not because I was training for anything specific, but because walking was the only thing that quieted my mind.

Movement kept the anxiety at bay. When I walked, my chest loosened. When I sat still, the questions pressed in: What am I doing? What comes next? How do I live without the identity I spent thirty years building?

I did not have answers. I only knew that if I kept walking, I could breathe.

I had stayed at The Standard before, drank at Claridge's, spent money I did not have trying to belong in rooms full of people who already did. This time, I stayed in a modest apartment and walked past those hotels without going inside. I sat in parks and watched people. I listened to my own thoughts without immediately trying to silence them.

For the first time in a very long time, I was not performing. I was simply being. And it was uncomfortable in ways I had not anticipated.

A train strike forced me to extend my stay. I welcomed it because it gave me more time to walk. More times to sit with the discomfort without numbing it. More times to let London teach me that I could exist in the world without a drink in my hand.

Before leaving Miami, I had been reading Richard Rohr's *Falling Upward*, a book about the transition between the first and second halves of life. Rohr describes the first half as the times when you build the container—you become focused on achievement, accumulate proof, chase security, do what is required to succeed by the rules you are given. The second half asks for something entirely different. It asks you to let go of striving and enter what he calls the sacred dance.

Most people do not make that transition willingly. Something has to fall apart first.

By the time I arrived in London, everything had fallen apart.

Fania was gone. Onda Mundial was gone. The career I had built my identity around no longer held me. I had no income and no plan. Sixty years of building a container had collapsed around me, and I did not know whether I had the courage to step into whatever came next.

Before leaving Miami, I rewatched *The Way*, the film starring Martin Sheen and his son Emilio Estevez about the Camino de Santiago—a thousand-year-old pilgrimage route across northern Spain where people from all over the world walk 500 miles seeking transformation, healing, or simply answers they can't find at home. I cried through half of it. A father dropping his son at the airport. A body claimed in a foreign country. Ashes scattered along a road. A man walking because he did not know what else to do.

What stayed with me most was not the plot but the truth beneath it. If you want to find yourself, you have to get off the merry-go-round. You have to leave the rat race. It will not be easy or pretty or even clear at first. But if you stay with it long enough, something real will eventually emerge.

Sitting alone in my Miami Beach apartment weeks earlier, I had known I needed to do this. Almost immediately, I felt terrified.

And now I was in London, still terrified, walking twelve miles a day because it was the only thing keeping me from falling apart.

Amsterdam: Staying Sober in the Noise

From London, I flew to Amsterdam to meet Michael, a friend I had known for fifteen years. We met during Pride, an experience I had never navigated sober.

Amsterdam Pride unfolds on the canals. Boats decorated in rainbows. Crowds lining the water. Music everywhere and beer flowing freely. I stayed with the designated driver and noticed how often my hand reached instinctively for a drink that was not there.

The pull was strong. For a moment, standing in the noise and color and celebration, I wanted to drink more than I wanted to stay sober. I played the tape forward—the hangover, the shame, the fragile ground of early sobriety cracking beneath me—and the desire passed.

But it did not pass easily.

Twenty years earlier, I had been in Amsterdam at a bachelor party and remembered almost nothing. This time, I saw the light on the canals, the brick buildings leaning toward one another like old friends, and the quiet dignity of a city that did not ask to be consumed to be enjoyed.

Michael thought I was crazy for planning the Camino. He had heard stories about bedbugs in *albergues*. I told him I did not care. I needed to do it, even though I was not ready. Even though I was terrified.

I needed to do something that required everything I had, something I could not numb my way through, something that would force me to meet myself honestly.

We flew together to Munich, where I stayed with Michael and his partner for nearly two weeks. One morning, Michael mentioned casually that I seemed slightly affected by Xanax. He was right. Alcohol was gone, but I was still reaching for something to soften the edges.

I made a mental note. First the Camino. Then that too would need to change.

Training: The Body Remembers

By the time I reached Rotterdam in mid-August, I was walking ten to twelve miles daily along the canals. My body adjusted quietly. Each morning I asked what it could handle, and each evening I noticed that the answer was often more than I expected.

Walking became a form of listening, not exercise, not training but medicine. And it was while sitting in a café in Rotterdam that I finally made the decision to do the Camino.

Anxiety softened when I moved. Depression loosened its grip when my body remembered rhythm. For the first time in my life, I was treating walking not as a means to an end, but as the thing that kept me present in my own skin.

I flew from Amsterdam to Bilbao and started training on its hills, four miles up and four miles down each day. My legs learned what climbing meant. The hills humbled me and taught me patience. I took breaks when I needed to and stopped apologizing to myself for doing so.

San Sebastián brought the ocean. Eleven miles a day along the coast. The horizon widened, my shoulders dropped, and the nervous energy I had been carrying since leaving Miami began to loosen.

I realized then that I was holding multiple emotions at once. Fear. Anxiety. Excitement. Hope. All at the same time. The walking did not resolve those contradictions. It made space for them to coexist.

That felt new. And honest.

I had committed without knowing whether I was ready. I worried about climbing the Pyrenees, the mountain range along the borders of Spain and France. I convinced myself that starting in Pamplona at the base of the Pyrenees in Spain was strategic rather than fearful. It was probably both. Simply put I didn't think I could make that first day walk on the Camino Francés from Saint-Jean-Pied-de-Port, France, to Roncesvalles, Spain.

The truth was, I did not know what the Camino would give me. I did not know if it would answer my questions or just make them louder. I only knew that I could not keep living the way I had been—rudderless, unmoored, waiting for someone or something to tell me what came next.

I needed to walk toward something, even if I did not yet know what it was.

On August 30, 2022, I walked my first true Camino day from Zubiri to Pamplona, still as a training day and not a real day on the Camino. The theme that arrived that morning was love, and I carried it with me through the day without fully understanding why.

Two days later, on September 2, I stepped out of my hotel in Pamplona and began walking.

There was no ceremony. No starting line. No one was waiting.

Just a path, a body that had learned to trust itself again, and a quiet willingness to begin.

I did not know who I would be on the other side. I only knew I could not stay who I was.

CHAPTER THREE: A LOVE STORY AND SELF-COMPASSION

By the time I left Puente la Reina on September 4, I had seen Bill three times in three days.

The first time was outside Pamplona. I was walking uphill in the morning heat when a cyclist came toward me, moving fast down the path. As he passed, I caught his face—the shape of it, the set of his jaw, the way his eyes looked through me rather than at me—and my breath stopped.

My brother Bill.

Not literally. The man was a stranger, probably European, mid-fifties, wearing gear that cost more than my entire pack. But the resemblance was so striking that I turned and watched him disappear down the trail, my chest tight with something I could not immediately name.

The second time was in a café. I was drinking coffee, studying the map for the day's route, when a man walked past the window. Same build and walk. Same face that looked exactly like the brother I had not spoken to in years.

I sat there staring at my coffee, trying to make sense of what was happening.

The third time was on the trail itself. Another cyclist, different gear, different age, but there it was again—Bill's face, Bill's energy, Bill's presence delivered to me three times in three days by men who were not him.

The Camino does not whisper its messages. When it wants your attention, it delivers them clearly.

I kept walking, thinking about my brother. About the apartment in Phoenix where I had tried to help him after his divorce. About how I could not save him. About how we had stopped talking without ever knowing how to begin again. About the thirty years of distance that had grown between us, built on things we never said and wounds we never named.

The message felt obvious enough. I needed to reach out to my brother.

But I was not ready. Not yet. I needed to keep walking and let the Camino continue doing its work.

The Daily Grind

The stretch from Pamplona to Logroño is where most pilgrims find their legs. It is where the body begins to understand what is being asked of it, where blisters either form or do not, where muscles adapt or rebel, and where your gear reveals whether it will support you or slowly undo you.

For me, it was the daily grind of walking until my feet screamed, arriving in town barely able to make it from the restaurant to my room, and collapsing into bed wondering whether I could do it all again the next day.

And then, somehow, I would wake up the following morning fine. My feet worked. My body was ready. I even felt eager to start.

The Injinji toe socks and Brooks trail runners were the right choice. They kept blisters away. At sixty years old I was in better shape than I had expected. The long months of training before the Camino—especially the climbs in Bilbao and San Sebastián—were paying off.

The walking poles were another story.

I had bought them in Pamplona during that frantic last day before starting, running around town trying to prepare for something I did not yet understand. I used them exactly once, on the descent from Alto de Perdon, the steep rocky path where everyone warned about twisted ankles and falling.

After that, they stayed strapped to my backpack, throwing off the balance and creating a sharp, persistent pain in my left shoulder. Every morning I told myself the pain would pass. It never did. Every evening I considered leaving the poles behind and talked myself out of it. I had paid for them. I might need them later. What if the terrain got worse?

I carried them for nearly a week, the pain intensifying daily, before I finally admitted what I already knew. I was holding onto something that hurt me simply because I had invested in it.

During those early days I also learned that, while I spoke with other pilgrims at rest stops and in towns, for the most part I walked alone. That solitude turned out to be necessary. The themes that arrived each morning, the memories that surfaced, the feelings I had spent decades numbing with alcohol—all of it required silence and space.

The endless golden fields stretching toward the horizon. The sky so blue it looked painted. The path rising and falling in gentle waves. It needed to be just me and the trail and whatever wanted to rise up from inside me.

Joe and his group were still around. Jasmine, Jeff, and Sam appeared now and then, and we shared meals occasionally, but we were no longer walking together. The Camino has its own rhythm. People come and go, and you walk with someone only when it is time to do so.

Emma

I met Emma in Los Arcos.

There was only one restaurant open in the main plaza, and as I sat there talking to Jasmine about the heat and my plan to leave early the next morning, a woman at the next table overheard me.

"I'm staying in the same guesthouse," she said, her voice clear and direct. "Can I walk with you tomorrow morning?"

I looked up. She was older than me, maybe mid-seventies, fit and lean, with gray hair pulled back and eyes that looked like they had seen a lot and decided most of it was worth smiling about.

"Sure," I said. "I'm leaving at 5:30, before sunrise."

"Perfect," she said. "I'll be ready."

The next morning, when I stepped outside in the dark, she was already waiting.

We stopped at the only café open for coffee and a pastry. Los Arcos looked entirely different in the early light—quiet and ancient, the stone buildings glowing soft orange in the streetlamps, the plaza empty except for us.

"I love this time of day," she said as we walked toward the edge of town. "Before the world wakes up."

"Me too," I said.

We started walking. Emma was seventy-four years old and remarkably strong. She walked fast, especially on the pavement, and I had trouble keeping up. For the first hour we moved mostly in silence, our trail runners finding rhythm on the path, the sky slowly lightening from black to deep blue to pale gray behind us.

As the sun rose, we began to talk.

She told me about her education—six different degrees, including both law and arts degrees, which felt like a perfect contradiction. Logic and beauty lived comfortably inside her.

I told her about Fania, about the music industry, about trying to figure out what came next now that the container I had spent thirty years building had collapsed.

"That's why you're here," she said simply.

"Yeah," I said. "I think so."

We walked through fields of harvested sunflowers, the stubble crunching beneath our feet. The path stretched ahead, endless and unchanging. The sun climbed higher. My legs burned but kept moving.

It was a long day. Twenty-eight kilometers to Logroño. By late afternoon, my feet ached and my shoulders hurt and I was ready to be done.

That's when Emma asked if she could share how her husband had passed.

"Of course," I said.

We slowed our pace. She took a breath.

"We met on a flight from Chicago to Boston," she began. "Both of us were divorced. Both of us were dating other people."

I listened.

"He was a fighter pilot who flew missions in Vietnam. By the time the plane landed, we went home, ended our other relationships, and began building a life together."

Her voice was steady, factual, but underneath I could hear something else. Not sadness exactly but perhaps gratitude. The kind that comes from having loved someone completely.

"We married and lived on the water in Maine. Early in our marriage, he was diagnosed with cancer—Agent Orange exposure from the war. But not before we had become, in my words, a couple of equals who inspired each other deeply."

The path curved through a vineyard. Grapevines heavy with fruit stretched in neat rows on both sides of us.

"About a year before he died, we renewed our wedding vows," she continued. "At sunset in our yard overlooking the Atlantic. Just his daughter and his best friend were there. We read our vows, kissed, and shared a small cake. His daughter recorded it on her phone."

I could picture it. The light golden. The water behind them. Two people who knew exactly what they had.

"The following year was difficult as his health declined. Eventually he was placed in hospice. Upstairs in our home."

She paused. I did not speak. I just walked beside her and listened.

"On one of his final good days, he asked to have a barbecue. Invite his daughter and best friend over. He came downstairs, ate, and laughed. Then he went back upstairs when he could no longer manage."

Her voice stayed even.

"Not long after, the hospice nurse called everyone upstairs. His daughter sat beside the bed and started playing the video of the vow renewal on her phone. I tried to stop it. I thought he might not want to see that moment. But he stopped my hand."

Emma's eyes were wet but she did not cry.

"He died watching the video," she said quietly. "Watching us say our vows."

We stopped walking. I could not speak for a long moment.

When I finally could, I said, "That's the most beautiful love story I've ever heard."

It remains so to this day.

We walked the rest of the way to Logroño in silence, not because there was nothing to say, but because there was nothing that needed to be said.

Letting Go

We arrived in Logroño exhausted and deeply moved. That evening, over simple food at a pilgrim café, Emma told me she was leaving early the next morning.

"I have a reservation in the next town," she said. "Different pace than yours."

"I'm taking a rest day here," I told her.

"Good," she said. "You should."

We hugged goodbye outside the restaurant. She held on a moment longer than expected.

"Thank you for listening," she said.

"Thank you for trusting me with that," I said.

I never saw her again, which is often how the Camino works. But I carried her story with me long after she was gone.

September 6 was my first rest day. Joe and his group had already left town, and when I woke up I felt sad and briefly regretful, wondering whether I should have skipped my rest days and continued walking with them.

By the end of the day, I was grateful.

I did laundry and got a haircut. I walked the city without a pack on my back. Ate lunch alone in a quiet plaza, watching people pass. I rested in a way I had rarely allowed myself to rest before.

The next morning, the shoulder pain was still there. The walking poles were still strapped to my backpack.

Near the door of the guesthouse was a bucket where pilgrims left their poles by the door. I stood there holding the poles, thinking about how long I had carried things that hurt me simply because I had paid for them or believed I needed them.

I placed the poles in the bucket and walked out the door.

By the next morning, the shoulder pain was gone.

Self-Compassion

Walking alone toward Nájera, with the sun warming my back and the weight finally lighter, a theme arrived.

Kindness and compassion.

At first it felt familiar. I had always believed those qualities were among my strengths. I was kind to people. I listened. I showed up. I helped when I could.

As the miles passed, that belief began to unravel.

Somewhere between Logroño and Nájera, walking through fields that smelled like dry grass and earth, I realized something uncomfortable.

I was not kind or compassionate to others. Not really, because I had never been kind or compassionate to myself.

You cannot give what you do not have.

The realization stayed with me most of the day. I saw how often I judged myself. How relentlessly I pushed. How quickly I turned to alcohol when I could not stand to be alone with my own thoughts. I had confused endurance with strength and self-criticism with discipline. I had spent decades believing that being hard on myself was the price of achievement.

Emma's story returned to me as I walked.

You cannot inspire someone if you do not respect yourself. You cannot love someone fully if you are at war with yourself. You cannot offer genuine kindness to others if you deny it to yourself every day.

I arrived in Nájera alone that evening. Without walking poles. Without my Camino family. Without Emma.

But with a new understanding that I could not give to others what I had never learned to give myself.

Even today, when I catch myself judging someone, I stop and ask whether I have been kind and compassionate to myself that day. Most of the time, the answer is no. And that is where I begin.

Just for today, I will not drink, smoke, use Xanax or poppers with you.

I love you, Michael and Mike.

And I move onward and forward in the grace of God.

CHAPTER FOUR: TO THE BONE

I walked out of Burgos and into the Meseta, the high-altitude plateau covering the heart of Spain, on a morning so cold I could see my breath hanging in the air.

The landscape flattened and emptied as the vineyards disappeared and the hills fell away, leaving nothing but horizon. The path stretched ahead in a straight line that seemed to have no end, gravel crunching beneath my trail runners, the sound carrying in the silence like a metronome marking time.

Cold mornings arrived before sunrise with my jacket zipped tight and my breath visible in the predawn darkness. By noon the heat came, ruthless and clean, pressing down until the ground shimmered and sweat soaked through my shirt. There was no shade and nowhere to hide, only gravel beneath my feet and wind moving through harvested fields that smelled like dust and memory.

Each morning before sunrise, I put George Winston's *Autumn* on my headphones and let it set the pace. The piano was spare and steady, never rushing me or asking for anything, giving me permission to move slowly and meet the day without bracing for it. Those first steps in the cold became a quiet ritual, the notes marking time as the land opened up around me, and by the time the sun rose, my body had already found its rhythm.

Most pilgrims hate the Meseta. Some endure it. A few fall in love with it.

For me it felt like recognition—the outer landscape finally matching the inner one, wide and exposed, stripped bare in a way that allowed me to stop running and begin to listen.

The Deep Dive

What pilgrims call the Meseta is really two things at once.

It is a physical landscape—endless plains, red earth, harvested fields stretching toward infinity, small medieval towns appearing suddenly out of nothing like mirages that turn out to be real.

But it is also an emotional landscape, a stretch of the Camino where the relentless sameness of the terrain strips away distraction and forces you to face whatever you have been carrying. There is nowhere to hide on the Meseta. No mountains to climb that make you feel accomplished. No beautiful coastline to photograph. No vineyards or forests to soften the monotony. Just you and the path and whatever rises up from inside you when there is nothing left to look at but yourself.

The towns are small. Most have one bar, one restaurant, maybe a small church. By evening, pilgrims gather in stone courtyards and narrow dining rooms, drinking wine because there is nothing else to do, talking because the silence of the day has left everyone raw and ready to confess things they would not say anywhere else.

I did not drink, but I sat with them anyway, listening to stories spill out—divorces, deaths, addictions, regrets, the reasons people walk five hundred miles to find something they lost or never had. The Meseta does this. It opens people up and makes strangers tell the truth.

And walking alone through those endless fields day after day, I began my own deep dive.

All the things I had spent decades avoiding rose to the surface—foster care, coming out, the devastation I had caused, the uncle who died alone, the family who asked me to disappear. The Meseta offered no distractions, no way to numb or sidestep or outrun any of it. Just miles and miles of walking with nothing to do but finally, finally look.

What surprised me was not the pain of remembering. It was the peace that came with it.

For the first time in my life, I was not running from these memories or drinking them away or burying them under achievement and motion. I was walking through them, one step at a time, letting them rise and settle and release. The rawness was real, but it was not unbearable. In fact, it felt like grace.

I began to understand that I did not need to relive these things again. I only needed to acknowledge them, name them, and let them go.

The Red Earth

The red earth began to look like Arizona, and with it came the ghosts.

I was thirteen years old when the judge decided my future. The judge's chamber's was smaller than I had imagined, paneled in dark wood that made everything feel closed in. My mother sat on one side, John beside her—my stepfather, the man whose fists and belt had taught me that home was not safe. I sat alone on the other side with a court-appointed advocate I had met only once. She smelled like cigarettes and cheap perfume and kept checking her watch like she had somewhere more important to be.

Judge De Rose looked down at the papers in front of him and then up at me. His face was kind but tired, like someone who had made this decision too many times before.

"Michael," he said, his voice flat and official, "I'm awarding custody of you to the state of Arizona."

I do not remember exactly what I felt at that moment. There may have been relief. There was certainly fear, but what I remember most clearly is the quiet that followed, the way the room seemed to be empty of sound even though people were still moving and talking around me.

My mother did not fight it. John said nothing. The decision had already been made before I walked into the judge's chambers.

What I learned that day was not that the system had failed me. I learned that I had already been surviving on my own for years and no one had noticed until it became a legal problem. Home had not been safe long before a judge said so.

I moved into my first foster home that afternoon. I do not remember the family's name or the color of the walls or what I ate for dinner. What I remember is the feeling of being untethered, of understanding that nothing was permanent, and that survival meant paying attention, staying useful, and not taking up too much space.

Foster care taught me that I had already been taking care of myself long before anyone acknowledged it. It taught me that being good, competent, and helpful could buy temporary safety, though that safety was never permanent. It taught me that adults could not be trusted to stay, that promises meant nothing, and that the only person I could rely on was myself.

I carried that lesson into adulthood. It made me exceptional at reading rooms and anticipating needs. It also made intimacy nearly impossible.

Walking through the Meseta, I said it out loud to the wind.

"It was not my fault."

The words came out quiet at first, almost a whisper, as if I were testing whether they were allowed.

"It was not my fault."

Louder this time, more certain.

"It was never my fault."

The fields stretched endlessly on both sides of me. The sky was so blue it hurt to look at, and nothing answered back. But something in my chest loosened anyway.

Coming Out

More than twenty years later, in 1991, I told my wife the truth.

We had been married for two years—two years of her calling me "her suit," the man who looked right, fit right, made sense on paper. Two years of her trying to save something that was never going to work no matter how hard either of us tried.

She knew, though she never said it directly. I could see it in the way she looked at herself in the mirror, pulling at her clothes, asking if she looked okay, wondering out loud if she should lose weight. As if her body were the problem. As if being thinner or prettier could somehow change what I was.

It broke my heart to watch her try to fix something that had nothing to do with her.

I had been on the East Coast for work, trying to reach her for days. Phone calls went unanswered and messages disappeared into silence. The knot in my stomach tightened with each attempt until I finally booked a flight home, knowing something had to give.

It was evening when I arrived at our apartment in Scottsdale. The Arizona heat was finally breaking, the sky turning that particular shade of purple it only gets in the desert. I unlocked the door and found her sitting on the couch in the dim light, waiting.

I had rehearsed the words for weeks, practiced them in my car, in hotel rooms, lying awake at three in the morning staring at unfamiliar ceilings. None of the practice mattered. When I finally said it, the words came out wrong anyway.

"I'm gay," I said. "I can't do this anymore. I need to leave."

Everything that happened next happened fast.

She started crying immediately—not quiet tears but deep, body-shaking sobs that filled the room. She stood up and grabbed my arm, her fingers digging in hard enough to leave marks.

"No," she said, her voice breaking. "No, no, no. We can work through this."

"We can't."

"Yes we can!" She was yelling now, still crying, her face red and wet. "I can change. I can be different. Just tell me what you need. Please. Please don't do this."

"It's not about you," I said, trying to pull my arm free, trying to stay calm even as my own chest tightened. "I can't—"

"Don't leave me. Please don't leave me."

I went to the bedroom and started packing, threw clothes into a suitcase without folding them, grabbed my toiletries, moved through the apartment like I was already a ghost. She followed me, kept crying, and kept begging.

"I love you," she said. "You're my suit. You're my person. We can fix this. Just stay. Please just stay."

When I zipped the suitcase and picked it up, she grabbed it, pulled at it, and tried to take it from me.

"Don't go. Don't go. Don't go."

I pulled back and she held on. We stood there in this terrible tug-of-war over a suitcase that represented the end of everything we had tried to build together.

"I have to," I said, my own voice breaking now. "I'm sorry. I have to."

She let go of the suitcase and grabbed me instead, her arms around me, her face pressed against my chest, sobbing so hard I could feel her whole body shaking.

"I can be thinner," she said into my shirt. "I can be prettier. Just tell me what to do and I'll do it. I'll do anything."

"It's not about that," I said, trying to untangle myself gently, trying not to hurt her more than I already had. "It has nothing to do with you."

But she would not let go.

I had to peel her arms off me, physically remove her hands from my jacket. It felt like the cruelest thing I had ever done. At some point I realized that she had broken her hand by hitting the wooden French doors to the balcony.

I picked up my suitcase and walked toward the door. She followed me, still crying, still begging. Down the stairs of our apartment building she came behind me, pulling at my suitcase, pulling at my arm, saying my name over and over like it was a prayer that might bring me back.

"Please. Please. Please."

I made it to my car and put the suitcase in the trunk. She stood on the sidewalk watching me, her face destroyed, her hands empty at her sides.

I got in the car.

As I pulled away, I saw her in the rearview mirror walking back toward the building.

I knew her hand was broken.

I drove to my friends Jill and Steve's house and told them they needed to go help her. They left immediately without asking questions, and I sat in their living room alone, shaking, knowing I had just destroyed someone I cared about simply by telling the truth.

Later they confirmed what I already knew—her hand was broken in three places.

The Voicemails

The calls started the next night.

Each morning when I arrived at my office, the message light was blinking. Sometimes there were two messages, sometimes five, sometimes ten. But they were always the same.

"I'm going to kill myself."

Her voice was calm, almost conversational, as if she were telling me about her day or asking me to pick up milk on the way home. She described how she might do it—pills usually, sometimes the car in the garage. She told me it was my fault. She said she could not live without me. She said I was her suit, her person, the only thing that made sense. Then she hung up.

I listened to each message alone with the door closed, deleted them, tried to work, tried to function, tried to convince myself that I could not save someone who did not want to be saved.

The calls went on for weeks.

I tried ignoring them, tried not checking my voicemail. But they kept coming, relentless and calm and always the same threat delivered in that eerily pleasant voice.

Finally, I called her back.

"I will get you all the help you need," I said, my own voice shaking with something between anger and exhaustion and grief. "I will pay for therapy. I will make sure you have support. But if you kill yourself, that's on you, not me. I can't carry that."

The line went quiet.

"Do you hear me?" I said. "I can't save you from this. You have to save yourself."

She hung up without saying anything.

The calls did not stop immediately but tapered off slowly, like an IV drip running dry. By the time I moved to Atlanta months later and the divorce was final, they had finally stopped altogether. The voicemails were gone, but the guilt remained.

Conversion Therapy

Her church offered a solution before I left Arizona.

They paid for conversion therapy. Her minister recommended it personally, told her it could fix me, that if I just tried hard enough I could choose to be different.

Part of me still believed it too. Part of me still thought that being gay was something I had chosen, something I could un-choose if I wanted it badly enough, if I prayed hard enough, if I suffered enough.

The therapist was kind but certain. He had an office in a strip mall, decorated with inspirational posters and a cross on the wall. He spoke gently but with absolute conviction, the way people do when they believe they are saving you.

He gave me rules.

I was only allowed to masturbate to thoughts about being with a woman—no men, no fantasies that involved what I actually wanted, just women. He gave me a list of approved websites showing straight pornography. He told me to condition myself, to train my body to want what it was supposed to want.

He told me that if I followed the program, if I really committed, I could be normal. I could go back to my wife. I could have the life I was supposed to have.

I tried.

I sat in my apartment alone at night, following his instructions, forcing myself to watch images that did nothing for me, thinking thoughts that felt like lies. I told myself it was working. I told myself I was getting better.

It did not work.

The Rehab

Eventually, I ended up in a rehabilitation center.

Not for being gay, but for childhood sexual abuse trauma—the thing underneath everything else, the wound that had been festering since I was seven years old.

The therapists there were different. They did not try to change me. They asked me what had happened and then they listened. They helped me see that the shame I carried was not mine to carry, that what had been done to me was not my fault.

At the end of the program, I made a decision.

I was going to move to Atlanta. I was going to come out. I was going to start a new life as the person I actually was, not the person everyone needed me to be.

It felt like stepping off a cliff.

My Uncle

At the same time all of this was happening, my uncle was dying.

He was gay and had AIDS. He was wasting away in a hospital bed while the family whispered about his lifestyle and avoided visiting him.

This was the late eighties, when hospitals treated AIDS patients like lepers. Nurses wore double gloves and masks to enter his room. His meals were left on trays outside his door. Some staff refused to touch him at all. The fear was everywhere—in the way people stepped back when they heard his diagnosis, in the hushed voices, in the wide berth everyone gave his room at the end of the hallway.

I went to see him once.

The hospital smelled like disinfectant and something else I could not name—something sterile and final. A nurse pointed me toward his door without looking at me, her hand wrapped in latex, her face carefully neutral.

When I walked in, I barely recognized him.

He had been vibrant when I was younger—loud laugh, quick wit, always moving, always alive. He was a beautiful man with stunning features including a thick mustache. Now he was small and gray, his body folded in on itself beneath thin white sheets. Machines beeped steadily beside the bed and an IV dripped something clear into his arm.

We did not talk about what was happening to him. We did not talk about me or about the family or about the silence that surrounded both of us. We just sat together in the fluorescent light and the sound of machines, two gay men carrying the same truth in different ways, in a room where fear had convinced people that even touching the doorknob might kill them.

He died three weeks later and I couldn't even come out to him.

The day after his funeral, my brother called.

"You can't be gay," Bill said, his voice matter-of-fact, as if he were correcting a simple mistake. "We're here to procreate. That's the whole point."

"It's not a choice," I said.

"You need to make it one."

We did not speak again for years.

The Guilt That Followed

For years—decades, really—I carried what I had done to her.

Not the leaving, because the leaving was necessary. But the way I had left. The devastation I had caused. The woman who had loved me so completely that she chased me down the stairs begging me to stay, who tried to physically stop me from walking out, who broke her own hand when I left anyway.

I never wanted to hurt someone like that again, so I did not let anyone get that close.

I dated and had relationships, but I always kept one foot out the door. I always left before it got too serious, before someone could call me their suit, before I had to look at another person and watch them fall apart because loving me was not enough.

I told myself I was protecting them. Really, I was protecting myself from ever again having to peel someone's arms off me while they begged me to stay.

It made me good at beginnings, terrible at middles, incapable of endings that did not involve disappearing before anyone could hold on too tight.

Even now, walking through the Meseta thirty years later, I carried the sound of her voice saying "please" over and over. I carried her hands pulling at my suitcase. I carried the image of her standing on the sidewalk watching me drive away. I carried the belief that loving me meant eventual devastation, and that the kindest thing I could do for anyone was keep them at a distance.

Peace in the Rawness

But something shifted as I walked those endless miles through red dirt and harvested fields.

The memories came, one after another, relentless and unavoidable. Including foster care, the courtroom, John and coming out. And finally the broken hand, voicemails, and conversion therapy. My uncle dying alone. My brother's rejection. All of it rose to the surface in the vast emptiness of the Meseta, and I could not outrun it or numb it or bury it under work and motion.

I could only walk through it.

And in the walking, I found something unexpected.

Peace.

Not the absence of pain, but the quiet knowledge that I did not have to relive any of this again. I did not have to keep carrying it like a weight that proved I was broken or unworthy or dangerous to love. I could acknowledge it, name it, let it move through me, and then let it go.

The rawness was real, but it was not unbearable. In fact, it felt like grace.

In the small towns at night, I sat with other pilgrims drinking their wine while I drank water or beer 0.0. I listened to their confessions and sometimes offered my own. The Meseta had opened all of us, stripped us down to what mattered, and in that shared vulnerability

I found something I had not expected.

Belonging.

Not because I had hidden my wounds, but because I had finally stopped pretending they were not there.

The Woman with the Coke

One afternoon, miles from anything that resembled a town, I came upon the only structure I had seen all day—a concrete table beneath a corrugated metal roof, planted in the middle of the plain as if someone had decided that one small mercy was enough for this stretch.

A woman sat there alone beside a cooler, her posture relaxed and unhurried. She looked up when she saw me and smiled.

I dropped my pack and sat, grateful for the shade and the invitation.

She opened the cooler and handed me a cold Coke. The condensation was already slick against my fingers and felt extravagant in that landscape, like receiving something I had not known I needed until it was offered.

She spoke quickly, her Spanish musical and shaped by a Galician cadence that rose and fell faster than I expected. I answered easily, surprised by how natural it felt after years of living in Mexico.

She stopped mid-sentence, studied me, and said how well I spoke Spanish. She asked where I had learned.

"Bolivia," I told her. "And later Mexico."

She nodded, satisfied, and continued speaking.

We talked about the Camino, the heat, the silence of the Meseta. Eventually the conversation softened into something looser and then into nothing at all, just two people sitting in the shade while the wind moved through the fields and the metal roof clicked as it expanded in the sun.

When I stood to leave, she wished me a *Buen Camino* and handed me another Coke for the road.

I understood her perfectly, and she understood me.

Boundaries

One night at a long communal table, laughter and wine loosened into confession.

Trauma spilled out and someone misheard a word. Anger replaced sorrow. Another bottle opened, and pain and alcohol began speaking the same language, voices rising, tears mixing with accusations that had nothing to do with what was actually being said.

I sat there watching it unfold, feeling the energy shift from connection to chaos, and I knew I did not need to stay. This was not my pain to carry and these were not my wounds to heal.

I stood up, said goodnight, and walked outside into the cool dark.

The next morning, clarity arrived with the sunrise. I understood that none of it was mine to carry, that boundaries were not walls but grace with a backbone. That I could care about people without absorbing their chaos. That walking away from dysfunction was not abandonment—it was self-respect.

In the days that followed, self-respect became the quiet refrain beneath every step, showing itself in small decisions. Asking for what I needed. Honoring the answers when they came. Protecting peace as fiercely as I once protected chaos.

The Towns

The towns appeared suddenly, rising out of the emptiness without warning.

One moment there was only road and sky, the next, church towers appeared, stone houses clustered around a plaza, voices drifting toward me in the breeze.

I always arrived exhausted, my body spent in a way that left no energy for performance.

As evening settled, everything softened. The light turned honeyed and shadows stretched across plazas. Locals emerged to sit on benches as if answering an unspoken bell. Children ran in slow circles. Dogs lay at their owners' feet. Pilgrims drifted in quietly, dusty and relieved.

Dinner was simple and generous. Pilgrim menus appeared like small gifts and I ate slowly, grateful for food that tasted honest and earned.

A German couple told me the Meseta was their favorite part of the Camino because it was honest, because you could not hide from yourself there.

Each night, I wrote in my journal, repeated my mantra, and slept deeply. My body trusted rest because the walking had been true.

Joy

Then joy arrived, sudden and uninvited.

The road was endless, the sun brutal, my feet worn. A song came through my headphones—one of those defiant gay anthems from the nineties, full of brass and glitter and unapologetic queerness.

Something inside me cracked open.

My body moved before my mind could stop it and I started dancing right there on the path, in the middle of nowhere, in the blazing afternoon heat. I laughed into the sun, spinning, arms out, alive in motion.

A young man on a bike pulled up beside me, concerned on his face.

"Are you okay?" he asked in broken English. "I thought you were collapsing."

I assured him I was fine, better than fine. He rode away slowly, looking back twice to make sure.

I kept laughing and kept dancing.

A year earlier, I had been on my couch in Miami, drinking myself numb, unable to imagine a future that did not hurt. Now I was dancing in Spain, sober, laughing, and unmistakably alive.

Held

The Meseta stripped me down and handed me back to myself.

I saw the boy from Globe who survived. I saw the man still walking, sixty years old, sober, exposed to the bone.

As I walked, the darkness softened and the horizon revealed itself slowly. Shadows became shape and shape became distance. The land unfolded patiently, as though it were allowing me time to adjust. I was not entering a place so much as being received into it.

When the sun rose, it did so gently, warming the ground beneath my feet and settling into the folds of the landscape. I turned off my headlamp and continued walking, aware of how small I was and how safe I felt at the same time.

My body relaxed without instruction and my breath deepened without effort. I felt held in a way that required no explanation.

The Meseta did not ask me to interpret it or improve myself within it. It offered no narrative and demanded no performance. It allowed me to move forward exactly as I was—tired, uncertain, stripped of pretense—and met me with quiet steadiness in return.

I understood then why this stretch unsettles so many pilgrims. When nothing is offered to lean on, you are left with yourself, and whatever you are carrying has nowhere to hide.

I kept walking, knowing I would not leave this place unchanged.

Just for today, I will not drink, smoke, use Xanax or poppers with you.

I love you, Michael and Mike.

And I move onward and forward in the grace of God.

CHAPTER FIVE: CRUZ DE FERRO

The climb to Cruz de Ferro began before sunrise.

I left Astorga in the dark, my headlamp cutting a narrow path through the predawn chill. The temperature had dropped overnight and my breath came out in clouds that hung in the beam of light before dissolving. My trail runners found purchase on the gravel road as the path began its steady ascent toward Foncebadón.

This was the climb into the high mountains of León—ancient, steep, unforgiving in its beauty. The kind of landscape that makes you earn every step.

By the time the sun rose, I was already deep into the climb, my legs burning, my pack riding comfortably on my shoulders. At the bottom of the pack, wrapped in a bandanna, were three small stones David had given me before I left Miami, knowing about the Cruz de Ferro tradition, knowing I would need to leave something on that mountain.

"For when you get there," he had said, pressing them into my hand. "You'll know what to do with them."

I had not thought much about it in Pamplona or on the Meseta or through any of the long days between. The stones stayed wrapped in the bandanna, quiet and patient, waiting.

The path rose steadily, the terrain becoming more barren as I climbed higher. Occasionally when looking back, I could see the valley below—the medieval walls of Astorga growing smaller behind me, the landscape opening into rolling plains that stretched toward the horizon. The morning light turned everything gold.

I was not thinking about Cruz de Ferro. I was just walking, one foot in front of the other, watching the path unfold.

Then suddenly, there it was.

The path opened onto a high ridge, and rising out of the earth like a prayer stood Cruz de Ferro—the Iron Cross. A weathered wooden pole maybe twenty feet high with a simple iron cross at the top, planted in a massive mound of stones. Thousands of them—maybe millions—left by pilgrims over the centuries. The mound rose ten feet high, a cairn built by generations of people who had walked this path carrying their own weights.

It happened so fast.

I had not realized I was this close. I thought I had more time, more distance, more opportunity to think about what I would leave here. But the mountain had arrived, and I was standing in front of it, and there was no more time to prepare.

I dropped my pack and sat on the ground, breathing hard, my legs shaking from the climb. The wind moved through the high grass around the cross, carrying the smell of sun-warmed stone and wild thyme. The silence was enormous.

I reached into my pack and pulled out the bandanna. Unwrapped it slowly and two of the stones fell out, warm from being carried against my back for two weeks.

What am I leaving here?

The question arrived with clarity and urgency. This was the place. This was where pilgrims left what they could no longer carry. David had given me these stones knowing I would need them, trusting me to know what to release.

And suddenly, I knew.

James and Robert

They had been my business partners at Fania for more than fifteen years.

When Robert hired me as chief marketing officer, the Fania catalog had just come out of probate—a legendary Latin music label that had created salsa in the sixties and seventies, then died and sat in legal hell for nearly a decade. Robert got it out of probate. That was his genius.

What I did was resurrect the brand.

For fifteen years, I rebuilt Fania from the ground up. We digitized the catalog, remastered albums, created remixes, launched club nights, celebrated the fiftieth anniversary in Central Park. We brought the music and the brand back to life.

They never quite believed in what I was doing. They let me do it—maybe because they did not have better options, maybe because the results kept coming—but they never truly believed in the cultural work, the brand-building, the long game I was playing.

When the company sold years later, the difference between the floor price and the ceiling price was thirty-five million. The investors said it was the brand—the story we told, the resurrection we led—that created that value.

I had asked for equity early on. Robert told me he would not ask for it on my behalf.

When the deal closed, I walked away with a management payout—a thank-you check that felt both generous and insulting at the same time. The brand work I had done created all the value. I got a fraction of it.

But that is a story for later.

What mattered now, sitting on this mountain with two stones in my hand, was that I had spent fifteen years with partners I thought would be with me until retirement. Partners I believed in even when they did not quite believe in me. Partners I had carried—their skepticism, their silence, their refusal to fight for my equity—like stones in my pack.

And I was done carrying them.

The Mountain

I stood and walked to the mound, holding the first stone.

It was small, white, ordinary—the kind of stone you could find on any path. But it felt heavy in my hand, weighted with years of waiting for validation that never quite came.

"I know what I built," I said out loud to the wind. "I know the value I created. I don't need you to tell me anymore."

I placed the stone carefully among the others and stepped back.

It felt like setting down a suitcase I had been carrying up steep stairs for fifteen years.

Then the second stone.

I placed the second stone on the mound.

The weight in my chest loosened.

I understood then that this was not about James and Robert being bad people. They had done what they could within the limits of what they understood. What mattered was that I finally valued myself enough to stop needing their validation. I knew what I had built. I knew my worth. I did not need them to confirm it anymore.

I turned away from Cruz de Ferro and started down the mountain, the third stone still wrapped in the bandanna at the bottom of my pack.

The Descent

The path down was steep and rocky, demanding attention with every step. My legs were tired from the climb, and I moved carefully, placing each foot deliberately on the uneven ground.

About halfway down, I caught up with two pilgrims I had seen at breakfast that morning—Leslie and Andrew, a couple from Australia walking their first Camino together.

Andrew was in his fifties, fit and steady, with the quiet confidence of someone who had learned to trust his body over the years. Leslie was about the same age, with an easy smile and an openness that made conversation feel natural from the first word.

We fell into step together, and the conversation flowed the way it does when people are walking the same path and no longer need to perform.

Andrew told me about his work, his love of hiking, the way the Camino had already changed something in him even though we were only halfway through. Leslie talked about their decision to walk together, the challenges of sharing such an intimate experience, the joy of seeing her husband discover something new in himself. What struck me the most is the happiness with which they walked the Camino.

I told them about the stones I had just left on the mountain. Not all the details, just the shape of it—business partners, fifteen years, times to let go.

They listened the way pilgrims listen—without judgment, without trying to fix anything, just receiving the story and holding space for it.

By the time we reached the bottom of the mountain, we had become a Camino family.

We would walk together off and on for the next week, sharing meals, comparing stories, laughing at getting lost along the path through medieval villages that seem untouched by time.

But in that moment, descending Cruz de Ferro with two strangers who felt like old friends, I understood something I had not quite grasped before.

The Camino does not just strip you down. It also builds you back up—not with the things you left behind, but with what you find along the way.

I had climbed the mountain carrying fifteen years of waiting for validation.

I descended carrying nothing but my pack, two new friends, and the quiet knowledge that I was enough.

The Third Stone

That evening in the rural house, unpacking my gear, I found the third stone still wrapped in the bandanna at the bottom of my pack.

I held it in my hand, feeling its weight, its smoothness, the way it fit perfectly in my palm.

David had given me three stones. I had used two.

I wrapped the remaining stone carefully and placed it back in my pack, knowing I would carry it until I understood what it was meant for.

It would be three years before I walked the Camino again, before I would place that final stone on a yellow arrow marker along the trail and understand that it was not a burden I was releasing but a gift I was returning.

Thank you, David, for knowing I would need them. Thank you for trusting me to know what to leave behind.

The path leveled out as we approached the next town, and I could see the church tower rising above the trees. My legs were tired but steady. My pack felt lighter. The sun was warm on my shoulders.

Andrew said something about finding a place for lunch, and Leslie laughed at a joke I had already forgotten.

We kept walking.

Just for today, I will not drink, smoke, use Xanax or poppers with you.

I love you, Michael and Mike.

And I move onward and forward in the grace of God.

CHAPTER SIX: O CEBREIRO

The morning I rode a horse up to O Cebreiro, I had completely forgotten I was supposed to.

Two weeks earlier, Donna, a fellow pilgrim, had told me about Victor—a local man who owned horses and would take pilgrims up the steep climb to O Cebreiro instead of making them walk. She gave me his email address and I wrote to him that same day.

"I have one horse left for that day," Victor replied. "It's yours."

Then I promptly forgot about it.

The Camino has a way of filling your attention completely—the walking, the themes that arrive each morning, the conversations, the exhaustion, the small miracles of finding food and a bed at the end of each day. A horse ride two weeks in the future felt abstract, distant, unimportant.

The day before the ride, it came back to me suddenly. I was sitting in my hotel room in the evening when I remembered—tomorrow morning, the horse, Victor, O Cebreiro.

I found Victor's email and wrote to him quickly: "Am I still on for tomorrow?"

"Yes," he wrote back. "It's yours, please be here tomorrow at 9:30."

The next morning I woke early, had breakfast, arranged for my bag to be transferred to the next town as usual, and walked to the meeting point Victor had described.

There he stood beside four horses saddled and waiting, their breath rising in clouds in the cool mountain air. Three other pilgrims were already mounted or preparing to mount. I was still in shock by the fact that there were only four horses and one was for me.

Victor looked at me and gestured toward the fourth horse as if I had been expecting all along.

"You ready?" he asked in Spanish.

I nodded, walked to the horse, and climbed into the saddle.

The moment I settled into the leather, something shifted.

My body remembered before my mind did—the feel of leather beneath me, the weight of reins in my hands, the solid warmth of the horse's back, the slight forward lean as the animal prepared to climb. My legs found their position without thinking. My hands knew how to hold the reins with just enough tension to guide without forcing.

I had not been on a horse in decades, but my body had not forgotten.

We started up the mountain, the horses moving slowly and steadily over the rocky path, their hooves finding purchase on the uneven ground.

And immediately, the landscape changed.

After weeks walking through the Meseta—flat, barren, endless fields under relentless sun—the mountains of Galicia felt almost overwhelming. Green everywhere. Trees thick and tall on both sides of the path. Creeks running clear over smooth stones. Clouds moving through valleys like living things. The air smelled like pine and damp earth and the faint musk of horse sweat.

The morning light filtered through the trees, turning everything soft and golden, and the beauty of it—after all that emptiness, all that exposure—was almost too much to hold.

I rode in silence, letting the rhythm of the horse's gait settle into my bones.

And that is when Buster arrived.

Buster

I had not thought about Buster Mounce in years. I had not let myself think about him, maybe, because the loss of that man—the one who had been my father in every way that mattered—was too much to carry on top of everything else.

But riding that horse up the mountain, feeling my body remember skills I learned when I was nine years old, Buster came back to me with such clarity it felt like he was riding beside me.

The stockyards in Globe, Arizona. The smell of hay and manure and dust. Buster in his straw hat and pressed western shirt with pearl snaps, teaching me how to sit a horse properly—back straight, heels down, hands steady but soft. Teaching me how to rope, how to work cattle, how to be useful when everything else in my world told me I did not matter.

Buster was my father, not by blood, not by law, but by everything that counts.

My real father abandoned us right before I was born. My stepfather was not a father—he was something else, something I am still trying to name. But Buster saw me when I was invisible. He gave me work when I needed a reason to survive. He taught me I was capable when every other adult in my life either ignored me or hurt me.

When foster care tried to take 4-H away from me—the one thing I had, the one place I mattered—Buster fought for me. I do not know what he did or who he called, but within weeks the rules changed and I could raise my steer.

When I was sixteen and won a scholarship to Bolivia, terrified and excited and desperate to escape Globe, Buster was dying of cancer. I wrote him a letter from South America—thanking him for everything, telling him what he meant to me, trying to say I love you in words that felt too small for what I owed him.

They read it at his funeral.

I came home a year later and he was already in the ground.

And I never grieved.

Not at sixteen when I got the news. Not at seventeen when I came home. Not in the forty-six years since.

I just moved on. The way you do when survival requires forward motion.

But riding that horse up the mountain to O Cebreiro, the memories flooded back—not gently, not in pieces, but all at once like a dam breaking.

Buster's hands adjusting my grip on the reins. His voice calling auction chants across the stockyards. The blue ribbon on my steer's halter. His grin lighting up the whole fairground. The way he told me, "The big cities—Chicago, New York—they're waiting for you," when he knew I was gay and knew I was not made for ranches and knew I needed permission to leave.

The kindest thing anyone ever said to me.

We rode up that mountain for four hours. Four hours of climbing through green mountains and thick trees and creeks running cold over stones. Four hours of my body remembering what Buster had taught me and my heart finally letting itself feel what I had been holding for forty-six years.

By the time we reached O Cebreiro, I was crying.

Quiet tears, steady the way grief comes when you have been holding it for half a lifetime.

O Cebreiro

We reached the top just as the clouds broke and sunlight flooded the mountaintop village. The place felt ancient and holy in a way that had nothing to do with architecture and everything to do with presence. Stone houses with thatched roofs clustered around a small church, the whole village perched on the mountain like it had grown there naturally over centuries. A woman was driving her small herd of cattle through the center of town.

I needed help getting off the horse.

Victor came over, steadied me as I dismounted. My legs barely worked and for the first time on the Camino, I almost could not walk.

And I was okay with that.

Because I had finally taken the time to process what Buster had given me. I had finally let him back into my life after forty-six years of keeping him at a distance because the grief felt too big to survive.

I thanked Victor, stood there for a moment breathing in the thin mountain air, and let my legs remember how to hold me.

Even now—years later, sitting here writing this—I often ask myself, "What would Buster do?"

When I do not know which way to go. When I am afraid or when I need to remember that I am capable of more than I think.

Buster is still with me. Not as a memory, but now as a presence.

Riding up that mountain, I dedicated the ride to him. Not out loud, not with words, just a quiet internal acknowledgment that this moment—this unexpected gift of being on horseback again after all these years—belonged to Buster Mounce and the nine-year-old boy he saved before that boy even knew he was drowning.

Thank you, Buster. You gave me worth when I had none. You gave me work when I needed a reason to live. You saw me when I was invisible.

You saved me before I knew I needed saving.

And you are still saving me.

The church bells rang, calling pilgrims to the pilgrim's mass.

I followed the sound.

The Pilgrim's Mass

The church of Santa María la Real was small and dim inside, the stone walls cool even in the afternoon light. Wooden pews filled quickly with pilgrims—dusty, tired, quiet. We had all walked hundreds of kilometers to get here, and the collective exhaustion in the room felt like a shared prayer.

The priest entered quietly. He was young and attractive with kind eyes and the unhurried movements of someone who had given this blessing thousands of times but still believed in its power.

He welcomed us in Spanish, his voice warm and resonant in the small space, and then he began to speak about the Camino.

"*Ultreia*," he said, letting the word settle in the air.

It is the historic pilgrim's cry, he explained. The ancient greeting pilgrims have called to one another for centuries as they walked this path.

"*Ultreia*," he said again. "Forward. Onward. Beyond."

He paused, letting each word land separately.

"*Más allá*," he said in Spanish. "The same meaning. Beyond. Over there. More ahead."

His voice grew stronger, more insistent.

"*Ultreia* is a powerful encouragement to keep going," he said. "To overcome challenges. To reach higher—spiritually and physically. The Camino teaches you this: Life is *más allá*. Always beyond. Always more over there."

He gestured toward the door, toward the path that would lead us down from this mountain and onward to Santiago.

"You do not walk to arrive," he said. "You walk to keep going. *Ultreia*. *Más allá*. There is always something beyond what you can see from here. The pilgrimage teaches you to trust that. To walk toward it even when you cannot name it yet."

I sat in that pew, my body still vibrating from the horse ride, my mind still holding Buster's face, and the priest's words landed in me like stones dropping into still water.

Ultreia.

Más allá.

Forward. Onward. Beyond.

My life was not back there—not in the broken marriage, not in the Fania payout, not in the childhood trauma I had spent the Meseta processing. My life was not even here, in this beautiful moment on a mountaintop in Galicia.

My life was over there.

Beyond what I had done. Beyond who I had been. Beyond what I could see from where I was standing.

The Camino was teaching me to keep going. To overcome what felt impossible. To reach higher, spiritually and physically, toward something I could not yet name but could feel waiting for me *más allá.*

The priest blessed us and gave each of us a small rock with a yellow arrow on it, which I still carry with me today. The mass ended.

I walked outside into the evening mist and understood that something had shifted.

O Cebreiro was the end of the spiritual part of the Camino for me. The deep dive was complete. The Meseta had stripped me bare. Cruz de Ferro had released what I no longer needed to carry. Buster had reminded me that I had always been capable, even when I did not know it.

Now the Camino was offering me something else.

An invitation.

Keep going. There is more. Your life is beyond.

The Final Hundred Kilometers

That evening, I sat outside my hotel with a cup of tea, watching the sun set over the mountains, and I understood that the Camino was changing.

Sarria, a historic town in Galicia, in northwestern Spain, marked the final hundred kilometers to Santiago. From here, the path would be more crowded—pilgrims joining from Sarria who only needed to walk the last hundred kilometers to earn their Compostela, or certificate of completion. The quiet solitude of the Meseta was over. The deep spiritual work was complete.

What remained was the walk itself.

One hundred kilometers of putting one foot in front of the other, trusting that the yellow arrows would lead me where I needed to go, believing that my life—my real life, the one I had not yet lived—was waiting somewhere beyond.

I thought about Buster teaching me to ride. About the priest saying "*Ultreia. Más allá.*" About the yellow arrow stone in my pocket. About the third stone still wrapped in my pack, waiting for its moment three years from now.

And I understood that the Camino had done what I needed it to do.

It had stripped me down. It showed me what I had been carrying. It had invited me to release it. And now it was showing me the way forward.

Not back to Miami. Not back to Fania or failure or the version of myself I had been trying to hold together with alcohol and deals and motion.

Forward. Onward. *Más allá.*

Beyond.

I finished my tea, stood, and walked back inside the hotel. Tomorrow I will walk to Triacastela and then Portomarín. Then one foot in front of the other until the spires of Santiago rose on the horizon and I stood in the plaza with my Compostela in my hand,

knowing I had walked five hundred miles to learn one simple truth:
  There is always something beyond.
  And the only way to reach it is to keep walking.
  Just for today, I will not drink, smoke, use Xanax or poppers with you.
  I love you, Michael and Mike.
  And I move onward and forward in the grace of God.

CHAPTER SEVEN: SANTIAGO

Everyone knows the Camino changes after Sarria. The last hundred kilometers—the minimum distance required to earn the Compostela—draw new pilgrims starting fresh, joining late, stepping onto the path with clean shoes and unmarked legs and excited voices discussing what lay ahead.

The trail filled quickly. At times there were traffic jams and you couldn't help but stop and chuckle. Where before I might walk for an hour seeing only one or two pilgrims ahead of me, now there were dozens moving in steady streams. Groups formed on narrow paths. Walking poles clicked against stone in constant rhythm. Conversations in a dozen languages echoed through the eucalyptus groves. It no longer felt like the Camino I had been walking for three weeks but more like an adventure to Disneyland.

I reminded myself that this, too, was part of the journey. Reentry. Learning how to hold what you have found when the world grows loud again.

I set my theme for the final stretch: love and gratitude. That was what I would carry into Santiago.

Reentry

One evening after a thirty-kilometer day, I sat down for dinner in the dining room of a small boutique hotel. I had showered quickly, slipped into my sandals—the same ones I had brought from home and worn every night of the walk—and came downstairs exhausted and hungry.

The dining room was full. At a nearby table, two American couples were talking, their voices bright with fresh-start energy. They had clearly just begun in Sarria—clean clothes, unmarked shoes, excited voices discussing the route to Santiago.

Then I caught a smell and looked around, confused, before I realized it was coming from my own feet. My sandals. Three weeks of sweat, dust, and five hundred miles compressed into foam and rubber. The smell was unmistakable—ripe, organic, impossible to ignore. Even after showering my feet, my sandals or my feet both still stunk. I tried to tuck my feet beneath the chair, mortified.

One of the American women said to her companion, "I heard someone walked thirty kilometers today," the way you might talk about an impossible feat.

I almost laughed out loud. That was me, that someone, but I did not feel heroic. I felt tired and my feet smelled terrible.

That was a reentry. Being back in a world where people had not walked your road. Where they did not know what thirty kilometers felt like. Where they were just beginning their journey while you were quietly finishing yours. Where your experience, which felt monumental to you, was just background noise to them, even if they might chat about you over dinner. You are not special. You are just another pilgrim. One who happens to be carrying a lot of miles and very smelly sandals.

I finished dinner quickly, went upstairs, and left my sandals outside the door. They had earned the night off.

Walking with the Brits

Daniel and Liam had been with me since the Meseta.

I cannot remember exactly when we first met—somewhere in those endless flat stretches between Burgos and León—but by the times we reached the green mountains of Galicia, we had fallen into an easy rhythm together. Dinners in small towns. Rest stops where we compared notes about the day's walk. Long conversations about everything and nothing.

They were raising money for ALS, walking the Camino to honor a friend who had died from the disease. Daniel was the strong storyteller, the kind of presence that made you feel calmer just being around him. Liam was loud, funny, always ready with a joke or a story that had everyone at the table laughing.

He had started calling me Miami Vice somewhere around León. I never asked why. It just stuck.

They were hilarious and a lot of fun to be with, though not easy to keep up with. They walked fast, talked fast, moved through the world with an energy that made me feel both ancient and grateful to be in their company.

Over the weeks we had shared meals, traded stories, walked stretches of the Camino together when the pace matched and the silence felt comfortable. By the time we reached the final hundred kilometers, they felt like old friends.

And every day, Liam coughed with deep, rattling sounds that bent him forward, hands braced on his knees, hacking until his face turned red and his eyes watered. Then he would straighten up, wipe his mouth, light another cigarette, and keep walking like nothing had happened.

I never said anything to him about it. It was not my place, and I was still sneaking off to smoke myself, still reaching for that same slow self-destruction.

But watching him struggle, day after day, I felt a message land with uncomfortable clarity. This is where you are headed if you do not stop. I could see it. Liam twenty years from now. Oxygen tanks. Shortened breath. Lungs that would not work anymore because he had spent decades poisoning them. I could see myself following the same path. It wasn't twenty years, though—in fact, Liam would pass in three years.

The message felt clear, not harsh but rather honest. God's way of introducing me to what was next. Just Stop!

I made a decision right there. One year sober—October 11, my sober anniversary—I would quit smoking too. No more numbing. No more slow self-destruction. No more hiding from myself in smoke and chemicals.

Onward and forward.

The Final Stretch

The days blurred together in the best possible way. Walking, resting, simple meals and small rooms. Conversations with Daniel and Liam about everything and nothing. The path became soft beneath my feet. My pack light as it had always been, just my few essential things and the stone David had given me.

My soul felt full again. Not happy exactly, but whole. As if something empty for years had finally begun to refill, one step at a time, one day at a time, one moment of presence at a time.

I thought about what I had done. I had stopped drinking eleven months ago. Stayed sober through holidays, loneliness, uncertainty, fear. I had turned sixty. Left Miami without knowing what I was looking for. I had just walked five hundred miles across Spain. Faced my past on the Meseta and left some of it on a mountain at Cruz de Ferro. And then I received grace on another mountain at O Cebreiro.

I had become someone I did not recognize when I started. Someone steadier. Someone who could sit with discomfort without reaching for a drink. Someone who knew his worth without needing anyone else to confirm it.

The night before Santiago, I stayed in a quiet country house outside O Pedrouzo. I was the only one staying at the house. After dinner I sat on the balcony as the sun dropped behind the green hills of Galicia. A cow mooed somewhere in the distance. Insects hummed in the grass. The air smelled like eucalyptus and the rain gave a dampness to the place.

Tomorrow I would walk into Santiago. The Camino would end, except it would not, not really. *Más allá.* Always beyond.

Dawn Departure

I woke before dawn on the final day.

I had walked most of the Camino alone, by choice and by necessity. The themes that arrived each morning, the memories that surfaced, the feelings I had spent decades numbing—all of it required solitude and silence.

But when I met Daniel and Liam at their hotel, Liam was waiting and smoking.

"Miami Vice," he said, grinning in the dim light. "You're not walking alone today."

Daniel appeared behind him, already packed, his headlamp switched on. I did not argue.

We left before sunrise, three silhouettes moving through the dark. The trail was quiet, just the sound of our steps and breath and the occasional rustle of animals in the underbrush. The sky moved slowly from black to deep blue to gray. We did not talk much because there was nothing left to say. We were walking into an ending that did not feel like an end.

After an hour the light began to change. The darkness lifted and the trees emerged from shadow, eucalyptus and oak draped in morning mist. Our headlamps became unnecessary and we switched them off, moving forward in the natural mist and light of dawn.

Somewhere around Lavacolla—the traditional place where pilgrims once washed before entering Santiago—we stopped at a small café. Daniel and Liam ordered beer even though it was barely ten in the morning. I ordered a 0.0.

We sat quietly, feeling the weight of what was about to change.

"One more hour," Daniel said.

"Less," Liam added. "Maybe five kilometers."

I looked at them and said, "Thank you for walking with me today."

"Wouldn't have it any other way, Miami Vice."

We paid and kept walking.

Monte do Gozo

The Hill of Joy. That is what Monte do Gozo means—the place where medieval pilgrims first glimpsed the cathedral spires of Santiago and fell to their knees in gratitude, knowing they had made it.

We climbed the gentle rise just after eleven in the morning. At the top, a large monument marked the spot, and beyond it, in the distance through the morning haze, I saw them. The spires. Two gray towers rising above the city, still kilometers away but unmistakable.

Santiago.

I stopped walking and Daniel and Liam stopped beside me.

"There it is," Daniel said quietly.

I stood there staring at those distant spires, feeling nothing and everything at once. I felt relief, exhaustion, disbelief, emptiness, and fullness at the same time. I had walked five hundred miles to see this view, and now that I was seeing it, I did not know what to feel.

We stood there for a long time, the three of us, not speaking, just looking at the place we had been walking toward for weeks.

Then Liam said, "Right. Let's finish this thing."

The Approach

The path led us down from Monte do Gozo and through the outskirts of Santiago. We walked along sidewalks now instead of trails. Cars honked. Buses rumbled past. People hurried by without noticing us, without knowing we had just walked across a country to get here.

We crossed a bridge and passed through neighborhoods where laundry hung from balconies and children played soccer in parking lots. Then, slowly, the old city began to emerge around us. Stone buildings, narrow streets, worn steps leading upward. The noise softened and the smell of old stone and incense drifted toward us on the breeze.

We followed the yellow arrows through winding alleys, past shops selling scallop shells and pilgrim staff, past cafés filled with pilgrims drinking beer at eleven in the morning, past churches where candles flickered in dark doorways. The streets grew narrower and the crowd thicker as we moved deeper into the old city.

Then we entered a tunnel, and I heard music echoing off the stone walls. A man stood in the shadows playing bagpipes, the sound mournful and triumphant at once, filling the tunnel with something that felt both ancient and immediate. We walked through toward the light at the far end, the bagpipes following us, and then we emerged into brightness.

Plaza del Obradoiro

The plaza opened before us and the cathedral rose massive and ancient, its stone facade weathered by centuries of wind and rain and prayer. The twin towers I had glimpsed from Monte do Gozo now stood directly above me, impossibly tall, impossibly beautiful.

The plaza was filled with pilgrims. Some wept. Others laughed. Many sat on the ground staring at their feet in disbelief, boots finally unlaced, blisters finally acknowledged. A few danced. One man lay flat on his back, arms spread wide, looking up at the sky.

Daniel and Liam stopped near the center of the plaza.

"We did it," Daniel said quietly, and we had.

The cathedral bells rang at noon. Pigeons lifted off the steps in a sudden rush of wings. The sun broke through the clouds and rested warm on my face.

Liam pulled out his phone and said, "Picture?" We stood together, the three of us, the cathedral behind us, and Liam's arm stretched out to capture the moment.

"To ALS research," Daniel said.

"To the Camino," Liam added.

"To getting here," I said, and the camera clicked.

Then they wandered off to explore the plaza, and I was alone again.

I walked to a low stone wall at the edge of the square and sat down. I watched the scene unfold around me—pilgrims arriving every few minutes, the same sequence of disbelief and joy and exhaustion playing out over and over. I watched people embrace. I watched them cry. I watched them stand in silence, staring at the cathedral like they could not quite believe it was real.

I had imagined this moment for weeks. I had expected something vast and conclusive. A sense of arrival. A feeling of completion. Instead, I felt tired, quiet, almost empty, and a little disappointed.

And then I understood.

I had not walked five hundred miles to arrive in Santiago. I had walked five hundred miles to become the person who could. The transformation had not happened here in this plaza. It happened on the way. Every morning I chose not to drink. Every day I walked sober and present. Every time a theme arrived and I let it in instead of numbing it. Every stone I left on a mountain. Every tear I cried on an empty road.

Step after step after step, the walking itself had been the healing. The journey was the gift, not the arrival.

There was no finish line. Only continuation. Just like sobriety. Just like life.

The plaza bells rang again. I sat there a while longer, letting it all settle. Then I stood and walked toward the cathedral.

Gifts from Home

That evening I returned to my hotel room and stopped in the doorway. On the small table by the window sat a bouquet of roses and a box of chocolates from Bryant and Lee.

I walked closer, confused, and picked up the card on the flowers. *Congratulations, Michael. We're so proud of you. —David*

I sat on the bed holding the card, feeling my chest tighten. My phone buzzed with messages from Chris and Mark, from other friends in Miami. People who had been following my journey, people who remembered, people who cared enough to send flowers across an ocean to a person they had not seen in months.

I lay back on the bed and cried. Not from sadness but from fullness. My soul was full.

The Pilgrim Mass

That evening the cathedral was packed for the Pilgrim Mass.

We arrived early but there were no seats left. Pilgrims filled every pew, lined the walls, and crowded the side chapels. Daniel and Liam and I found a spot near a stone pillar where we could see the altar, and we stood there as more pilgrims pressed in around us. We were dusty and tired, and our feet burned. We came from dozens of countries, spoke different languages, and carried different beliefs. But we had all walked the same road.

The priest entered and began the service in Spanish. I understood most of it. The words washed over me, familiar and strange at once. We stood through the entire mass, my legs tired from the day's walk but holding steady, and I did not mind. This felt right. Standing here among hundreds of pilgrims, all of us waiting for the same moment.

Then it came. The moment everyone was waiting for. The *botafumeiro.*

Eight men in red robes pulled a massive rope, and the giant silver thurible began to swing. Slowly at first, then faster, then impossibly fast—a silver blur swinging in huge arcs across the transept, smoke trailing behind it like visible prayer, the chains creaking with the weight of centuries.

Back and forth it flew, nearly touching the ceiling at the peak of each arc, the smoke filling the cathedral, pilgrims gasping and pointing and pulling out phones to capture something that could not be captured. The incense smell grew thick and sweet. The chains groaned. The thurible became a pendulum marking time and faith and the prayers of a thousand years.

It was magical. Exactly the pomp and circumstance we needed to finish the Camino. Not quiet or understated but grand and theatrical and unapologetically ceremonial. A spectacle that honored the magnitude of what we had all done, that said: This matters. You walked hundreds of miles and you deserve this moment of wonder.

I stood there watching it swing, feeling the weight of a thousand years of seekers pass overhead, and I knew I was one of them. I had walked the same road they walked. Carried the same questions. Sought the same answers—or at least the same peace.

The thurible slowed. The smoke thinned. The service continued. When it ended, we walked outside into the cool Galician evening and I understood that something had been completed. Not finished but completed and there was the difference.

The Compostela

The next morning I walked to the Pilgrim's Office.

The line stretched down the street—hundreds of pilgrims waiting to receive their Compostelas, the certificates proving they had walked the Camino. I took my place at the end and waited.

The line moved slowly. Pilgrims compared notes, showed each other blisters, exchanged contact information, and promised to stay in touch. Some would but most would not and that was okay.

Finally, I reached the counter. A woman looked up at me, her face kind but efficient. She had done this thousands of times.

"Name?" she asked in Spanish.

"Michael," I said.

She wrote carefully in beautiful script: *Michaelus*, the Latin version of my name, the pilgrim version.

She stamped the certificate, embossed it with the cathedral seal, and handed it to me.

I held it in my hands. Thick paper, official stamps, my name in Latin, the date, the confirmation that I had walked at least one hundred kilometers to Santiago. Except I had walked five hundred.

I started in Pamplona on September 2, 2022. I had walked through heat and cold, through vineyards and endless plains, over mountains and through forests. I had faced my past. I had left some of it behind. I had learned to walk *with* myself instead of running *from* myself.

This piece of paper was proof. Not proof that I had walked five hundred miles. Proof that I had become the person who could.

I bought a tube to put it in and slipped it into my pack.

Beyond

On the train to Madrid, Galicia slid past the window, green hills, slate roofs, vineyards climbing the mountainsides, small churches appearing and disappearing behind stands of eucalyptus.

I pulled out the yellow arrow stone from O Cebreiro and held it in my hand. It was smooth and flat. The yellow arrow was still visible despite weeks in my pocket.

I thought about the priest's words: *Ultreia. Más allá.* Forward. Onward. Beyond.

The Camino did not end in Santiago. It began there. Everything I had learned—about myself, about sobriety, about walking instead of running, about letting go instead of holding on—all of it was meant to be carried forward, applied and lived.

Más allá.

I did not know what came next. I had no job waiting in Miami. No plan. No clear path forward. But I knew who I was now. And I knew I could walk through uncertainty without drinking it away.

I put George Winston's *Autumn* on my headphones and closed my eyes. The piano was spare and steady, never rushing, never asking for anything. Just like the Camino. Just like the life I was learning to live.

One step at a time. Onward and forward. In the grace of God. Always beyond.

Just for today, I will not drink, smoke, use Xanax or poppers with you.

I love you, Michael and Mike.

And I move onward and forward in the grace of God.

PART TWO

AFTER THE CAMINO

CHAPTER EIGHT: THE 30-DAY LIST

Miami hit like a heat lamp when I stepped off the plane in late October. The air was thick and unmoving, the light harsh and fluorescent even at dusk. The taxi driver asked where I had been, saw my sunburned face and the scallop shell dangling from my backpack, and smiled knowingly without needing an answer.

My apartment looked exactly the same when I unlocked the door—the furniture arranged as I had left it, the hard sun pouring through the windows the way it always had. But I did not feel the same standing there. My soul was full. That was the message I had texted Kelly from Santiago: *I feel my soul is full again.* For the first time in years, I felt peace. Not the kind poured from a bottle or borrowed from a deal or someone else's approval, but the kind that comes from finally meeting yourself and liking who is there.

I unpacked slowly, deliberately, placing each object from the Camino on my nightstand like witnesses. The scallop shell. The yellow-arrow stone from O Cebreiro. A pine cone I had picked up along a Galician path. They sat there reminding me of what I had walked through, what I had left behind, and what I had learned. Everything felt different because I was different.

The List

In Sarria, after eighteen rainy kilometers, I had sat in a café and written out a plan on the back of a napkin that I later transferred carefully into my journal. I called it *30 Days*, though I knew even then it would take longer than that. It was my map for life after Santiago, a way to translate the Camino's lessons into daily Miami life.

The list was organized by category, each one representing a dimension of the life I wanted to build. Friends: Unity on the Bay, AA meetings, times with David and the few who really understood what it meant to start over at sixty. Work: reach out to old contacts, update LinkedIn, reenter the professional world I had left behind when drinking consumed everything. Spiritual: go where I actually felt God, not where I thought I should. Fitness: ten-mile morning walks, add swimming back into the routine. Health: doctor, dentist, whole foods, take care of the body that had carried me five hundred miles. Dating: put myself out there, stop hiding behind work and sobriety as excuses. Family: call Mom, have lunch with Owen, reconnect with Bill after thirty years of silence.

At the bottom, I had underlined twice: *Be kind, compassionate, respectful, and loving to yourself first. You cannot offer what you do not give yourself.*

The Camino had shown me who I was, and now I had to live it.

What Held

AA held from the beginning and became an anchor in those first weeks back. Burned coffee in Styrofoam cups, folding chairs arranged in a loose circle, a clock on the wall that never hurried anyone through their story. *Just for today* felt like something I could carry in my pocket, a promise small enough to keep. I went often enough to stay honest, often enough to hear my own story reflected back to me through other voices telling versions of the same struggle.

October 11, 2022, marked one year sober, exactly one year since the brunch with my nephew Owen and his fiancée where I had said true things in terrible ways because I was drunk. One year since my sixtieth birthday. One year since my last drink. I did not force celebration or make a big announcement. I gave it space, let it settle quietly, and it was held.

Swimming held too, becoming something I looked forward to instead of something I forced myself to do. I joined a gym with a pool and started going early, before the sun turned Miami into a furnace. Breath, stroke, turn, breathe. The water taught my body how to quiet itself again, how to move without urgency or performance. My nervous system remembered ease. At sunrise I walked the beach four to six miles, the Atlantic breathing beside me in steady rhythm. It felt like the Camino translated into sand and salt air, the same meditative movement carrying me forward one step at a time.

My friendships held in the way real friendships do when you stop performing and start showing up honestly. The people who stayed when I got sober and did not ask me to be anyone else. I stopped apologizing for leaving early or skipping bars or not drinking at celebrations. I simply lived the truth of who I was becoming, and the people who mattered understood. The people who did not matter drifted away quietly, and I let them go without guilt or explanation.

Family held, too, though it took longer to rebuild and required more courage than I had anticipated. The Camino had been clear about this on the Meseta when Bill's face kept appearing in strangers. *Reconnect with your brother.* In November I flew to California and met Bill for lunch at a restaurant near his house in the suburbs where he had settled after his own life had fallen apart and been rebuilt. It was not perfect, but it was real, a beginning we both needed even if neither of us knew how to say it directly. We talked about Globe, about our mother, about the years of distance that had grown between us built on things we never said and wounds we never named. We did not solve everything, but we started.

I met Owen, my nephew, for lunch in South Beach, just the two of us at an outdoor café where we could watch people pass and not have to hold eye contact through the hard parts. I slid a spare scallop shell across the table and told him to keep it for when he was ready to walk his own Camino, whenever that might be. Then I apologized for the brunch a year earlier, for saying true things the wrong way because I had been drunk and unable to see past my own pain to how my words might land on someone I loved.

He looked at the shell, then at me, and said simply, "It's okay. Thank you." Two sentences that held more grace than I deserved, acknowledging that the past could not be changed but that he saw me trying now and that was enough.

He kept the shell. Later that fall, he asked me to officiate his wedding in Mexico City in December. I said yes without hesitation, understanding that this was trust being offered, a chance to be present for something sacred instead of destroying it with alcohol and bad judgment.

These were the things that held in those first months back from Santiago. I gave them time and space and presence, showing up when I said I would, keeping promises I had broken a thousand times before. The Camino continued teaching me from five thousand miles away.

The Film Festival Job

The executive director role at the film festival looked perfect on paper when I found the posting in October. LGBTQ+ stories, community building, partnerships with local organizations, everything I cared about wrapped in a job description that seemed designed for exactly who I was becoming. I applied, interviewed across three rounds, and accepted the position in early December without doing enough research into the organization's actual health.

Within weeks, the cracks became visible in ways I could no longer ignore or rationalize. A dysfunctional board that could not agree on basic decisions. Messy finances that no one wanted to address directly. Leadership dynamics that made real progress nearly impossible, every meeting turning into performance instead of work. I remember sitting in a board meeting in January, listening to the same circular argument replay for the third time while nothing was decided and no one took responsibility for moving forward. I had an agenda in front of me, authority in my title, and no real permission to lead. That was the moment I understood that effort alone was not going to fix a structure that did not want to be fixed.

I showed up anyway through December and January and into February, running meetings, making decisions, carrying the festival forward as best I could with the resources and authority I actually had instead of what the job description had promised. But my voice began to crack more often, literally and metaphorically, my throat raw from tension and my spirit exhausted from pushing against resistance that would not budge. Integration has its own fatigue, I was learning. Even good habits feel heavy when life does not rush to meet your transformation.

In late March, after months of pushing against dysfunction that would not budge, I resigned. I left without bitterness or blame, sending the board a clear, professional analysis of what was not working and what needed to change if they wanted the organization to survive. I wanted to leave something useful behind, not another scar or story about how people had failed me.

The Camino had taught me that walking away is not failure, and sometimes it is the most faithful thing you can do. Sometimes you serve a place best by leaving it honestly instead of staying and slowly poisoning yourself with resentment.

The Voice and Smoking

Thirty years of cigarettes had left their receipt in my throat, and now the bill was coming due.

On calls and at events, my voice would break mid-sentence, forcing me to clear my throat and push through while pretending nothing was wrong. It was more than unprofessional. It was proof of the gap between who I wanted to be and what I was still carrying, every broken syllable reminding me I had quit alcohol but not everything that kept me numb.

I had promised myself in Sarria, watching Liam cough his way across Galicia, that I would quit smoking on my one-year sober anniversary. October 11 came and went, and I was not ready. November passed, then December and I kept making excuses, kept telling myself one addiction at a time was enough, kept sneaking cigarettes on my balcony like I was still hiding from judgment instead of my own fear.

In March, I finally tried. I bought nicotine patches and followed the instructions carefully, convinced this would be easier than quitting alcohol because I had already learned the method.

Days later my body went to war with itself in ways I had not experienced even in early sobriety. Panic attacks woke me at three in the morning, my heart racing so fast I thought it would break through my chest, my hands shaking, sweat soaking through my shirt and sheets. I called David in the dark, barely able to speak, convinced I was dying or losing my mind or both. One week of hell that made early sobriety feel manageable by comparison.

At the doctor's office, when he asked if I was using nicotine patches and I said yes, he nodded calmly and told me I was overdosing. I was not breaking down. My body was flooded with nicotine from both the patches and the cigarettes I was still sneaking when the cravings became unbearable, when I convinced myself that just one would not matter. He looked at me directly and said, "Don't let the OD go in vain. Just quit."

And I did.

I quit the patches that day. The panic faded within forty-eight hours, like someone had turned off a siren that had been blaring inside my chest since the week began. I smoked one last cigarette standing on my balcony, then crushed it in the ashtray and threw the rest of the pack in the trash along with the lighter and everything else that smelled like smoke and shame.

I quit the same way I had quit drinking—one day at a time, one hour when that was all I could manage. I woke up the next morning and did not smoke. Not forever, just for today.

Weeks became months, my voice steadied. People stopped noticing the breaks because there was nothing to notice anymore, the evidence of damage fading as my body slowly healed itself.

Two addictions, same method, same grace carrying me through when willpower was not enough.

The mantra had begun simply back in October 2021 when I first got sober: *Just for today, I will not drink with you.* When I quit smoking in 2023, I added that too. Then I looked honestly at what else I was using to numb the edges of discomfort and loneliness. Xanax when I could find it. Poppers when connection felt out of reach and I wanted to disappear into someone else's body instead of staying in my own. I added those as well, not as perfection but as intention, prayer before proof that I could actually do it.

Just for today, I will not drink, smoke, use Xanax or poppers with you.

What Did Not Hold

Work did not arrive the way I had hoped or planned when I made that list in Sarria. I made calls to old colleagues in the music industry, had coffee with new contacts in Miami's nonprofit scene, sent emails that went unanswered or got polite responses that led nowhere. Everyone was warm, encouraging, genuinely happy to see me doing well and looking healthy. But warm hellos were followed by polite silences and vague promises to stay in touch. No opportunities materialized. No doors opened. Miami is a beautiful city and an expensive waiting room where people with money wait for other people with money to decide what happens next.

Dating did not land either, though I tried harder than I wanted to admit. I went to fundraisers, small dinners, LGBTQ+ community events where I made small talk and had conversations that felt like auditions where I never quite got the part. I came home exhausted every time, wondering why something meant to be simple felt like performance, why I could not just be present with another person without calculating whether they liked me or judging myself for caring. The truth was I did not know how to date sober. I did not know how to be present with someone without alcohol smoothing the edges or numbing the fear of rejection.

By March, I was burning through savings faster than I had planned. The film festival job was over. Freelance work was sparse and unreliable. The apartment rent was crushing my budget. I could feel the familiar anxiety creeping back, the old warrior voice whispering that I needed to hustle harder, prove more, make something happen before the money ran out and I had to admit failure.

But the Camino had taught me something different. Sometimes you do not fight. Sometimes you adjust the path and trust that the yellow arrows will appear when you need them.

Arizona

Before choosing what came next, I flew to Arizona to see my mother in early April of 2023. I had not been back since getting sober. Part of me hoped things would be different now that I was different. Part of me knew better but went anyway, unable to let go of the fantasy that sobriety would somehow fix what sixty years had not.

John was still there. She was still with him. The house looked the same—the furniture arranged exactly as I remembered, the heat on, the silence heavy with things no one would say. The tension felt the same too, the way it had when I was thirteen and trying to stay small enough not to get noticed. I tried kindness with boundaries and lasted two days before I felt the old survival instincts kicking in, the ones that said: get small, stay quiet, do not make waves, do not give him a reason.

On the plane home, staring out the window at clouds that looked like the Meseta stretched across the sky, I finally wrote the truth I had been avoiding for years. I cannot save her. I cannot change him. I can only protect the boy who survived that house, the one who learned to disappear before the fist came down.

That was not selfish. It was survival.

The Decision

Back in Miami, I sat on my couch with a legal pad and ran the numbers in columns that did not lie. Stay in Miami and burn through my remaining savings within six months, or go somewhere cheaper and buy myself time—time to write, time to figure out what came next, time to let the transformation settle instead of forcing it into old patterns that no longer fit.

Spain tugged at me with memories of the Camino and the peace I had found walking those five hundred miles. But Mexico tugged harder for reasons both practical and instinctive. Lower cost of living that would stretch my savings. Real opportunities in the music industry through contacts I still had from my years at Fania. Owen's wedding in December, which gave me a concrete reason to be there and a deadline that made the decision feel less like running away. And something else I could not quite name yet—a sense that Mexico City might offer what Miami could not, a chance to start over in a place where no one knew the drunk version of me.

I was not running. I was choosing space and time and possibility. I was following the yellow arrows even though I could not see where they led.

The decision settled in my chest like something that had been waiting to be recognized. Mexico City. May through December at least, maybe longer. I would, explore the music industry opportunities, see what unfolded when I stopped forcing outcomes.

The Bittersweet Camino

I packed the scallop shell, the yellow arrow stone, and the pine cone from Galicia into a small box that would travel with me to Mexico City. Since getting sober eighteen months earlier, I had lost thirty pounds. I had walked five hundred miles across Spain. I had quit smoking after three decades of slow suicide. I had reconnected with my brother after years of silence. I officiated my nephew's wedding with a steady voice and clear eyes. I had tried at the film festival, failed honestly, learned what I needed to learn, and kept walking without bitterness.

I missed the Camino with an ache that surprised me—the arrows pointing the way forward, the rhythm of walking that made everything else quiet, the clarity of forward motion when life felt stuck. But the gifts kept arriving when I let them, appearing in small moments of grace that I would have missed if I had still been drinking or hustling or performing for approval.

One hour at a time. One honest conversation at a time. One clear *no* at a time when something did not serve the life I was trying to build.

The Camino was not behind me, finished and filed away as a story I told at parties. It was under every step, teaching me how to walk through ordinary life with the same presence I had learned on those five hundred miles through Spain.

Before leaving Miami for Mexico City, I updated the mantra one final times, adding the words that had become my compass:

Just for today, I will not drink, smoke, use Xanax or poppers with you.

I love you, Michael and Mike.

In the grace of God, I move onward and forward.

LESSON: THE 30-DAY LIST

The list I wrote in Sarria was never meant to be completed the way lists usually are, with neat checkmarks and a sense of accomplishment when everything is crossed off. Thirty days to rebuild a life that had taken decades to assemble and unravel was ambitious, maybe unrealistic, but the Camino had already taught me something more useful than ambition: You do not need to get everything right. You only need to keep showing up.

What I learned in those first months back was that integration is not the same as arrival. I had walked five hundred miles, quit smoking, reconnected with my brother, and officiated my nephew's wedding. The transformation was real. But transformation does not grant immunity from old patterns. It grants awareness of them, which is both a gift and burden.

Some things steadied themselves with surprising ease. Meetings. Swimming. Friendship. Those mornings felt familiar in my body, the way they had on the Camino when I laced my trail runners without debate. You woke up, you showed up, and you walked. The ritual mattered more than the outcome.

Other things did not hold despite my best efforts. Work fell apart. Dating felt hollow. Plans changed. And I learned that collapse is not the end of the road but another stretch asking you to keep moving when the view does not match the map you thought you were following.

What I could not yet see was that the list was not the point. The list was training, teaching me to orient myself each day by asking: What matters right now? Not what should matter, not what mattered yesterday, but what needs tending at this moment.

The cigarettes were the hardest to quit. That's why "I will not smoke" remains in my mantra years later. Not because I still smoked after the Camino, but because the promise to myself never expires. Some battles you win on the Camino. Some you win later, in ordinary moments of crisis back home. Either way, the commitment stays.

The Camino did not end in Santiago. It became the way I learned to walk through ordinary life—one day at a time, one honest choice at a time, with the understanding that change does not move in straight lines. It loops, doubles back, resists. Some days you walk with confidence. Other days you stumble. What matters is that you keep placing one foot in front of the other, trusting that the path is forming beneath your feet even when you cannot see where it leads.

And I kept walking.

CHAPTER NINE: MEXICO CITY

Through the airplane window in late May, Mexico City unrolled like a mirage, a valley of lights held in place by mountains that looked like sentries standing watch. Twenty-two years in Miami were behind me. Everything ahead was uncertain.

The landing was smooth. Immigration waved me through without questions. I caught an Uber into the city, watching neighborhoods slide past the windows as if I were being folded into something already in motion, something that had been happening long before I arrived and would continue long after I left.

It was a strange kind of comfort. I had been here before for Owen's wedding, for business meetings, for visits that always came with return tickets and end dates. This time was different. This time I was not passing through on my way to somewhere else. I was staying.

The Airbnb was in Roma Norte, a neighborhood of tree-lined streets and art deco buildings painted in fading pastels, cafés spilling onto sidewalks, young people on bikes weaving through traffic like they owned the place. I dropped my bags in the small apartment, opened the window, and let the city wash over me. Engines, voices, music bleeding from open windows. Life, loud and unapologetic and utterly indifferent to whether I could keep up.

I unpacked slowly, deliberately, the way I had learned to do since the Camino. The scallop shell. The yellow-arrow stone from O Cebreiro. The pine cone from Galicia. I set them on the dresser where I could see them every morning, the same ritual I had followed since returning from Spain. They sat like witnesses, reminding me of something I was already starting to forget.

I did not know whether I was running toward something or away from something. Maybe both. I had learned on the Camino that leaving does not always mean escaping, that sometimes it simply means beginning again somewhere else. But standing in that unfamiliar apartment with traffic noise filtering through the window, I wondered if I actually believed that or if I was just telling myself a better story about survival.

Torre Reforma

The next morning I woke at 5:30 without an alarm, my body still operating on Miami time, and walked to Torre Reforma. The gym sat twenty floors above the city, all glass and sky, with volcanoes visible on clear days when the smog lifted. I lifted weights, then swam laps in the pool, the water warm, the air cool, the view almost absurd in its beauty. From up there, Mexico City looked manageable, organized, like something I could understand if I just got high enough to see the whole picture.

Charly, the trainer I had met on a previous visit, waved from across the deck.

"You're back," he said in English mixed with Spanish.

"For a while," I answered, not sure how long a while meant.

"Good," he said, smiling. "We missed you."

I did not have a plan yet, but I showed up. Sometimes that was enough. The Camino had taught me that much at least.

After the swim, I grabbed breakfast in Polanco at a café where the coffee was strong and the chilaquiles arrived with perfectly fried eggs and salsa that made my eyes water. I opened my laptop and began sending emails, chasing the shape of something that had not yet decided to exist. A consulting project with a Mexican label, a digital media company in Mexico City and a joint venture with another marketing firm to host a conference on Latin music for brand. Each one felt possible until I hit send and the silence began.

The Hustle Returns

The projects moved slowly or not at all, while my savings evaporated like heat off the pavement in July. I knew what was happening. I chased several things at once because that was what felt familiar, what the hustler in me knew how to do. By noon most days I had sent twenty emails and felt more productive than I had in months, even though nothing was actually producing income. But knowing something and being able to stop it are two different things.

I told myself this was strategic networking, building relationships, planting seeds that would eventually grow into opportunities. Really, it was panic disguised as productivity. I did not know how to trust the process when the bank account was shrinking and no one was saying yes.

Back in Miami, I had subleased my apartment to my nephew and his business partner while I figured out Mexico. They had just opened an office nearby and needed housing. It seemed perfect when I arranged it—family, proximity, stability, everyone winning. Then the rent stopped coming.

My nephew and his partner had a falling out. The business faded. Every month I found myself chasing rent from thousands of miles away, trying to manage a problem I could not fix without damaging the relationship. It became heavy in a way I had not anticipated, this weight of trying to hold boundaries with family while also needing the money to survive.

I could not solve everything. But I could still take care of myself. That was what I told myself anyway, even as I felt things tightening around me.

Moving Around

I moved Airbnbs every few weeks when the monthly rates expired or when I convinced myself that a different neighborhood would feel different and somehow solve the loneliness that followed me like a shadow. Roma Norte. Condesa. Polanco. Then San Ángel, quieter and colonial, with cobblestone streets and slower mornings and bougainvillea spilling over stone walls.

San Ángel gave me space to think, but it also gave me too much silence, isolation that did not heal so much as echo. Moving days always hit me hard, packing everything I owned into two suitcases and a backpack, reminding me of exactly where I was and where I was not. Not settled. Not safe. Not sure this was working.

I walked every morning anyway, four to six miles along Reforma or through the tree-lined streets of Condesa where dogs and their owners moved in slow synchronized circuits. The rhythm helped. One foot in front of the other. The Camino translated into concrete and exhaust and street vendors selling tamales before dawn. But it did not feel the same. It felt like I was going through the motions, performing the ritual without accessing whatever grace had made it work in Spain.

I was lonely in a way that surprised me. Mexico City is enormous, filled with millions of people, and somehow I felt more isolated than I had walking alone through empty fields on the Meseta.

I downloaded Scruff, a gay dating app, again in September, deleted it a week later, and downloaded it again in October. It had been a coping mechanism for years, a way to feel connected when real connection felt out of reach. Now it felt like another weight, another habit I was ready to loosen but not yet ready to release. I did not know how to just sit with loneliness without trying to fill it. The wizard would sit with it, I thought. The wizard would trust that connection when it comes. But I did not know how to be the wizard when the loneliness felt like it might swallow me whole.

Missing the Camino

On September 2, exactly one year after I had started walking the Camino from Pamplona, I posted a photo from that first day. *One year ago today,* the caption said, but I wrote more in my journal that night. I would give anything to start the Camino again. To be back on that path with the yellow arrows showing me exactly where to go next.

The next day I wrote that I missed it deeply and wished I could go back and begin all over, walk it again with fresh legs and an open heart and no idea what was waiting at the other end.

I had learned the lesson on the Camino that the journey is the destination, that presence matters more than arrival, that trust is stronger than force. I knew all of that intellectually. But I was not living it. I was hustling again, juggling projects, waiting for someone to say yes so I could feel like I was doing something right.

Fear narrowed my vision. Hustler mode returned full throttle, convincing me that effort alone would solve everything if I just worked harder, networked smarter, and proved my value more clearly.

The scallop shell sat on the dresser watching me work myself into exhaustion. I looked at it some mornings and thought: I learned this. I walked five hundred miles to learn this. Why can't I live it?

But knowing how to walk a path and knowing how to live without one are two completely different things.

Zipolite

In late October, I flew to Zipolite, a coastal town along the Mexican coastline in the state of Oaxaca, and checked into a small Airbnb room with an ocean view and a hammock on the balcony where I could watch the sun set over the Pacific.

I spent two weeks, with no meetings and no emails chasing projects that would not close.

The beach was nearly empty, a crescent of sand framed by green hills and turquoise water breaking against rocks in steady rhythm. I swam, walked barefoot at sunrise, and let the days stretch without trying to fill them with productivity.

I made playlists, something I had not done since getting sober because music used to be too tangled up with drinking and drugs and nights I could not remember. One became my Top 100 Songs of My Life, each track a time stamp marking who I was at sixteen, twenty-five, forty, sixty. Sixty-two years compressed into music. I wanted to remember. To honor the road I had walked before it faded into the story I told myself about survival.

Fun no longer meant escape. It meant presence and it felt different in a way that mattered.

Some mornings I sat on the balcony with coffee and watched fishing boats move across the water, and I felt something loosen in my chest. Not permanently. Just for those moments. Enough to remember what the stage in life felt like even if I did not know how to stay there.

San Miguel de Allende

I flew to San Miguel de Allende for Día de los Muertos in early November of 2023. My comadre Michel and his husband John had a house there. I had married them years earlier in Miami, one of my favorite weddings, two people who loved each other without pretense or performance, who made vows and kept them.

San Miguel glowed during the holiday in ways that made my chest ache. Marigolds everywhere. Candles flickering in doorways and cemeteries. *Papel picado* strung across streets in bright geometric patterns. Music folding grief and joy into the same breath. Families gathered in cemeteries to tell stories and laugh with their dead, to remember them not as loss but as presence.

Walking through the Jardín one afternoon with Michel, he looked at me and said, "You seem different."

"I am different," I said.

"Good different or bad different?"

"I don't know yet," I admitted.

He smiled. "Fair enough. You'll figure it out."

That night, sitting in his courtyard under string lights with wine for them and sparkling water for me, I felt held in a way I had not in months. Loved without conditions or explanations. They did not need me to have my life figured out. They just needed me to show up, and I had.

Back in Mexico City in late November, I reconnected with Brad about the digital media company idea we had first discussed in Munich the year before. Carlos and I had refined the vision, rebranding it and widening the frame to include not just Mexico City coverage but a larger platform to reach Mexican and Mexican Americans, covering such topics and food, art, and music.

Brad's ex-husband David flew down from Chicago to see what we were building. We showed him the city the way you show someone a place you love—Teotihuacán at sunrise, the Zócalo at midday, street tacos at midnight, the National Museum of Anthropology on a quiet Tuesday when the crowds were thin. Then we pitched.

David asked hard questions and challenged assumptions. He stayed curious instead of skeptical and by the end of his visit, he was in, and ready to invest time and resources into making the company real.

Sitting at a rooftop bar after the final pitch meeting, watching the city lights spread out in every direction, I thought: Maybe healing looks like finally believing you belong in the room.

The Year Turns

I spent New Year's Eve alone on a rooftop in Roma, watching fireworks bloom in every direction, the sky above Mexico City turning into a war zone of celebration and light. I thought about the year behind me and the one ahead, more than two years sober now, still walking even when I did not know where the path was leading.

I was still sober. Still showing up. Still trying to figure out how to live the lessons I had learned on the Camino instead of just remembering them fondly from a distance.

I did not know what would work. I only knew what would not. Forcing. Proving. Hustling my way to worthiness. This had kept me alive for sixty years, but it could not teach me how to trust or how to believe in myself.

LESSON: MEXICO CITY

Returning to the hustle was the hardest thing I did in Mexico City, not because I wanted to but because I did not know how not to. Fear summoned this the moment my savings started shrinking and nothing was landing, because I knew how to survive and survival felt more urgent than transformation.

I knew intellectually that forcing and hustling and proving would not work anymore. The Camino had taught me that. But knowing something in your head and knowing it in your body are two completely different things.

Familiar patterns returned not because I wanted them to, but because familiarity still registered as safety in my nervous system. When the ground feels unstable, you reach for what your hands have held before even when your mind knows better.

Mexico City taught me that transformation is not a permanent state you arrive at and get to keep. You can forget what you learned. You can slide backward. The question is not whether you will fall back into old patterns but what you do when you realize you have.

The Camino does not disappear when that happens. It waits, quietly, offering another way to move through uncertainty when you are ready to choose it again.

The work was never about erasing the warrior. It was about learning when to let him stand down, and more importantly, learning how to actually live as the wizard instead of just talking about it.

Knowing the path and walking the path are not the same thing.

This, too, was part of the walk.

CHAPTER TEN: WARRIOR MODE

I forget the wizard first.

It happens quietly, without drama. The calendar turns from 2024 to 2025, and I am already moving faster than I mean to. I recognize the pattern, but recognition does not stop it. I am back inside the old machinery, watching myself accelerate even as I tell myself I know better.

The pattern repeats so precisely I almost miss it. Last New Year's Eve, alone in a temporary apartment in Roma Norte watching fireworks bloom over Mexico City, I was full of possibilities. This New Year's Eve—December 31, 2024—I am alone again in another temporary place, and the hope feels manufactured, rehearsed, hollow. The loneliness has teeth now, and instead of listening to what it is trying to tell me, I accelerate.

Christmas arrives quietly. I treat the day like a strategy document, scripting it carefully so the feeling will not count. Christmas Eve workout at Torre Reforma. City Market groceries for two days so I will not have to leave the apartment. A long walk to the Zócalo to prove I am still moving forward. A movie to fill the evening hours. If I plan it tightly enough, maybe the emptiness will not get in.

On Christmas Day I walk nine miles through neighborhoods that are quiet and shuttered for the holiday. I call my mother in Arizona, my comadre Michel in San Miguel, John in the States. Boxes checked. Back at the apartment, I open Grindr, close it, open it again.

That night I write in my journal that I am grateful to be in my own place and able to do whatever I want. Even as I write it, I know I am performing happiness rather than inhabiting it. I tell myself the rule is simple: stay sober. If I do not drink, smoke, or take Xanax, I am fine.

But fine is not a direction. Fine is not the wizard. Fine is just warrior armor polished to look like peace.

New Year's Eve arrives carrying the same hollowness. The lightness I felt the year before is gone. The Camino had taught me how to slow down, how to trust, how to choose wizard over warrior, but when I need those lessons most, I cannot reach them. I feel them slipping through my fingers like water, like yellow arrows I can no longer see.

David arrives from Miami just in time. We have dinner in Roma at a place with good wine for him and good mocktails for me, then walk Reforma as the city pulses around us preparing for midnight. Music spills into the streets. Strangers hug at midnight. Fireworks explode overhead. For a few hours, I am not alone.

The next morning he flies back to the States. I walk home through streets still glittering from the night before, and the silence hits harder than I expect.

January

January 2025 opens with my body staging a revolt. Too many poppers over the holidays leave me with a persistent upper respiratory infection that never quite resolves. I cough constantly. My chest feels tight. My body is asking me to stop, and I respond by pushing harder.

I landed a six-month lease in early January in the Reforma building I have wanted for years—floor-to-ceiling windows, views of the city spreading out in every direction, amenities that feel like arrival, like I have finally made it. Stability is the cure, I tell myself. A permanent address will fix what moving around could not.

Around the same time, Andres enters my life. He is younger, handsome, easy to be with in a way that requires no real vulnerability. It feels good to be wanted. I tell myself I am bringing my authentic self this time, showing up honestly instead of performing. But if I am being truthful, I am also using him to blunt the edges of being alone, the same way I used alcohol for thirty years.

The deals spin up again like they always do when I get scared: Pinal Music with Marco, our catalog acquisition company that feels perpetually on the verge of breakthrough. Pinto, the legendary Mexican label we have been chasing for months with terms sheets and meetings that circle without landing. PinkBox, a music tech startup that keeps saying yes without ever actually committing. Septo Música, the Brazilian label that pays invoices just often enough to keep me hoping.

My calendar fills with meetings, pitches, follow-ups, strategy sessions. On paper, momentum. Inside, my spiritual life becomes checkboxes—AA meetings attended, walks completed, journal entries written, gratitude lists compiled—items to complete rather than practices to inhabit.

The Camino taught me to slow down and instead I sprint.

It taught me to trust and instead I control.

It taught me to listen to my body. I stay sick and keep forcing myself forward.

Wizard over warrior, and I choose armor and speed every single time.

By January 5, I add poppers to the mantra and tell myself I am done with them. I quit one drug and replaced it with another. Work becomes my new fix. Every term sheet delivers a hit of proof that I still matter, that sixty-three years old and starting over was not a mistake, that I am still capable of building something that counts.

Andres and I settle into a rhythm—gym sessions at Torre Reforma, trips to Ikea to buy furniture for the new apartment, dinners in Polanco where we talk about nothing that matters. It looks like a connection from the outside. When jealousy surfaces because he is seeing other people and I pretend that is fine, I manage it so the arrangement keeps working. I do not ask whether either of us is actually getting what we need. The real clincher is we had moved from dating to carrying him now as an employee.

My journal keeps naming the truth without acting on it. I write that I am anxious and tired, that I need to get out of fight-or-flight mode, that I need to recharge my batteries. I track steps and switch to keto, measure inches lost around my waist, applying external fixes to internal problems the way the warrior always does.

Mid-January, Marco and I met with Pinto executives in their offices overlooking Polanco. Eduardo seems distracted, checking his phone while we present. Héctor is engaged, asks good questions, nods in the right places. They tell us they will get back to us. I leave energized anyway, convinced this is the one that will close. Septo Música pays an invoice a few days later, and the validation hits like sugar in my bloodstream. I write in my journal that I feel like I am getting my stride back, not knowing what is coming.

February

February arrives, and I declare the theme in my journal: gratitude. I mean it, and I also use it as protection. *My life has changed profoundly,* I write. *Thank you, God.* The sentences are true and also a shield. If I list blessings hard enough, maybe I will not have to say out loud that I am lonely, sick, and repeating a pattern the Camino tried to retire.

A weekend in San Miguel with my comadre Michel in mid-February is gentle and familiar. Saturday market buying vegetables and flowers. Noon AA meeting where I share honestly for the first time in weeks. Pizza with friends who have known me long enough to see through the performance. On Sunday morning, I go to see Paul.

We have been doing Friday breakfasts together for over a year now—strong coffee, chilaquiles, long conversations about everything and nothing. We disagree on almost everything political and like each other anyway. A month earlier, I brought him a space heater for his bedroom because San Miguel gets cold at night and his circulation is not what it used to be. Now he is in the hospital.

Paul looks smaller when I walk into his room. Older. The man who had seemed indestructible at breakfast tables is diminished by tubes and monitors. When he wakes and sees me standing there, he smiles and says my name. We hug carefully around the IV. We talk until the nurses come in to drain fluid from his lung, their efficiency making the moment ache with a closeness and finality I am not ready to acknowledge.

When they leave and close the door behind them, the room changes. Something settles in the air between us that feels like goodbye even though neither of us is saying the word.

I say it before I can stop myself, words spilling out to fill the silence: "You have so much to live for, Paul. So many people who love you."

Paul gives me a gentle half-smile and a small shake of his head. He was not angry or bargaining, just certain. He is not asking for encouragement or platitudes. He is telling me something I do not yet know how to hear—that he is ready, that he has made peace with what is coming, that my need for him to fight is about me, not him.

In the taxi back to Comadre's house, I feel empty and heavy at the same time. I nap for two hours. I go to a Grammys party that night at Steven and David's, to make small talk, network, and perform. I write four flat lines in my journal about the hospital visit and close with my mantra. Nothing pierces the armor.

Paul leaves the hospital shortly after. I tell myself he will bounce back the way he always does. I do not let myself know what I already know.

March

February blurs into March. Walks grow longer—eight miles, ten miles, twelve miles on weekends. Work accelerates. Numbers, proposals, planning sessions, term sheets that never quite close. Andres and I keep our routines going even though neither of us is happy.

The invitation from Eduardo at Pinto comes in early March.

A simple text asking whether I will attend the Feria Internacional de la Música (FIM) in Guadalajara. After weeks of waiting to hear back on the Pinto term sheet Marco and I submitted back in January, it feels like movement, like maybe the stalled conversation will finally begin again. Maybe we will meet face-to-face and close the deal that's been circling for months. I register, book my flight, and tell myself it will be a short trip.

By the time I pack for Guadalajara in early March, I am already half gone—exhausted, sick, running on fumes and force of will.

On paper, momentum.

In my chest, wobble.

I call it gratitude and keep moving.

FIM Guadalajara feels like the hinge I have been waiting for. A major music conference where every thread converges and every introduction leads to the next deal, the next opportunity, the next proof that I am still relevant. Validation arrives in the form of invitations—panels, meetings, dinners with executives who matter.

I am still coughing. Two months now. The infection never fully resolves because I never fully rest. I promise myself I will stop after FIM, after the deals close, after I have earned the right to be tired.

The night before I fly to Guadalajara, I rehearse pitches in my head lying in bed staring at the ceiling. All the deals that are almost there, almost closed, almost ready to prove that moving to Mexico City was not a mistake.

I think about walking nine miles on Christmas morning so I would not have to feel anything.

I think about Paul's quiet shake of his head.

I still cannot hear the message.

LESSON: WARRIOR MODE

The warrior returned because I forgot that transformation is not a destination you reach and get to keep. It is a practice you choose every day, and some days you forget how to choose it.

I knew the Camino's lessons intellectually, slow down, trust, and listen to your body. Choose presence over productivity. But when loneliness pressed in and savings dwindled and validation felt urgent, I could not access what I knew. The warrior stepped back into the driver's seat because survival felt more important than wisdom.

The hardest part was watching myself do it. I could see the pattern repeating—the hustle, the relationships used to numb loneliness, the work becoming addiction, the body staging revolts I ignored. I wrote about it in my journal. I knew better. And I kept doing it anyway.

That is the gap the Camino tried to close: the distance between knowing and doing, between intellectual understanding and embodied practice.

Paul tried to show me. His gentle shake of the head in that hospital room was not defeat. It was in fact acceptance. It was the wizard's wisdom I could not yet hear—that worth is inherent, not earned. That rest is not something you deserve after proving yourself. That peace comes from surrender, not achievement.

I was not ready to hear it. I was too busy running toward the next deal, the next proof, the next validation that would finally be enough.

The universe was patient. It waited until I had exhausted every warrior move I knew.

Then it stopped me.

CHAPTER ELEVEN: GUADALAJARA

Eduardo at Pinto had sent a brief message asking whether I would attend the Feria Internacional de la Música (FIM), and after weeks of silence on the term sheet Marco and I had submitted in January, I read more into it than was there. I told myself it meant the conversation might finally move forward, that a face-to-face meeting could close what had been circling for months. I registered, booked my flight, and framed it as a short trip. Wednesday to Friday, then back to Mexico City by the weekend.

I landed in Guadalajara Wednesday evening, convinced I was following momentum, and took an Uber to the Hotel Intercontinental. I planned to return to Mexico City by the weekend. After dropping my bags in a room that looked like every other business hotel I had stayed in over the years, I walked across the street to the mall for dinner. The city felt different from the moment I arrived. Not unsafe exactly, but unsettled. The air felt heavy, the energy restless in a way I could not quite place. I had spent time all over Mexico—Mexico City, San Miguel, Puerto Vallarta, Zipolite—but Guadalajara carried something else, something that sat on my skin and refused to leave.

I ate quickly at a chain restaurant where the food tasted like nothing and returned to the hotel.

That night I opened Grindr even though I knew better, even though I had written in my journal two days earlier that I needed to stop using hookup apps to fill the emptiness. Messages came in the way they always did. I chatted with a few men without any real intention of meeting, just distraction more than desire, a way to feel connected without the vulnerability of actual connection. A familiar pattern that still felt harmless even though I knew it was not.

The next morning I took an Uber to the university convention center. The conference was larger than I expected, filled with booths displaying album covers and artist photos, banners announcing new releases, panels on streaming economics and catalog valuations, faces I recognized from years in the business moving through the crowd making deals and taking meetings.

Almost immediately I saw the Pinto booth, and with it, clarity arrived like cold water. They had not invited me personally. They were sponsors of the conference. Eduardo's message had gone to his entire contact list—hundreds of people, maybe thousands. It was not a signal that he wanted to see me or move our deal forward. It was marketing.

I ran into him shortly after near the coffee station. He introduced me to his team and spoke easily about projects in motion, deals he was working on, opportunities he was exploring. At one point he mentioned, almost in passing, that he had a side deal going with Primary Musica on both catalog sales and artist buyouts he was managing privately, separate from anything we had discussed. It did not surprise me. That was how he operated, always running multiple streams, nothing clean or singular, never fully committed to any one path.

I attended a few sessions over the course of the day, took side meetings in hotel lobbies and hallway corners, and wandered the city between panels using a *New York Times* guide that promised insight into Guadalajara's emerging neighborhoods. Downtown felt uneasy in ways I could not articulate. The areas labeled cool felt constructed, beautiful surfaces with no depth underneath. I could not shake the sense that something was off, that the city was performing itself for tourists and industry people like me without ever inviting us in.

Friday morning I met Toy, a label owner from Monterrey I had worked with during the Fania years, for breakfast at a café near the convention center. Pablo, another industry friend, joined us. They spoke enthusiastically about the festival happening that weekend and urged me to stay an extra day, saying it would be worth it to enjoy the music.

I changed my flight from Friday evening to Sunday morning and booked a hotel closer to the festival venue. This was what momentum looked like, I told myself. Being able to stay flexible and available. Showing up when opportunities appeared.

Late Friday afternoon I returned to the Intercontinental to pack and check out before moving to the new hotel the next day. I was still on Grindr, still scrolling, when one conversation stood out from the background noise. It was clear, direct, easy in a way that felt different from the usual back-and-forth. We talked about meeting that evening. He suggested a few beers. I told him I did not drink but could have a Corona 0.0. He said that was perfect and mentioned bringing poppers for the evening. It felt oddly considerate, like he was trying to meet me where I was.

Normally I moved conversations to WhatsApp before meeting anyone, a small safety measure I had learned over years of hookups in unfamiliar cities. But this time I did not. Instead, I suggested we meet in the hotel lobby first so I could at least see him before going upstairs. He arrived looking like his photos, calm and friendly with an easy smile that put me at ease.

We went up to my room on the eighth floor.

We opened the beers—a Corona 0.0 for me, a regular one for him. We talked for a while about nothing in particular, the kind of small talk that happens before sex when both people know why they are there but need to ease into it. Then we had sex. It was good, familiar in the way anonymous sex becomes when you have done it enough times to know the rhythm.

Afterward he suggested I lie down while he gave me a massage and that we finish our beers. I lay down on my stomach and took another drink from the bottle on the nightstand.

That is the last thing I remember.

Saturday

I woke up Saturday morning around nine with my mouth dry and my head heavy in a way that went beyond exhaustion or dehydration. Something was wrong. I stood slowly and walked into the bathroom. In the mirror I saw a cut on my face near my temple and dried blood along my cheek that had crusted overnight.

Back in the room my phone was gone. My laptop was gone. My luggage lay open on the floor with the lock broken, clothes spilling out. The emergency cash I kept in a hidden pocket was gone. My passport remained, discarded on the bed like it had no value to whoever had been here.

I stood there in the silence trying to connect the pieces while the room seemed thick with chemical residue and shame pressing down on everything. I went downstairs to the front desk and attempted to explain what had happened. The words came slowly, my tongue thick, my thoughts scattered. The manager listened without expression and told me they had called the police and an ambulance, then asked for a relative they could contact in case of emergency.

The only number I had memorized was my mother's in Arizona. I told them not to call her. That she was ninety-two years old and could do nothing to help. They called her anyway and as I said she was not able to do anything.

I sat in the lobby waiting. After some time the manager returned and said the police and ambulance were not coming. They had tried several times but no one was available. He checked my account on his computer and reminded me that I was checking out that day, that my reservation ended this morning. He repeated it more than once. No one asked if I was okay. No one suggested a hospital. No one seemed concerned that someone had been drugged and assaulted in their hotel overnight.

I remembered I was supposed to have breakfast with Uchi that morning. I could not recall her phone number, but I remembered her hotel name. The front desk called and reached her. I asked them to tell her I needed help.

She came immediately, arriving within twenty minutes with one of the conference executives she had been meeting. They helped me pack my scattered belongings into the broken luggage and took me to the medical tent at the festival grounds. The medics cleaned my cuts with antiseptic that stung, checked me over for other injuries, and gave me medication for inflammation. There was no hospital visit offered and no police report filed. No one suggested testing for what I had been drugged with or checking for other damage.

The hotel had treated me like a problem to be resolved quickly and quietly. Uchi treated me like a human being who needed help.

She took me to the prepaid hotel I had booked for the weekend and gave me enough cash to cover a taxi to the airport the next morning. I fell into bed and slept for twelve hours straight, my body shutting down to process what had happened.

Sunday

Sunday morning I woke with just enough money for breakfast and a taxi to the airport. I ate mechanically in the hotel restaurant, showered carefully around the cuts on my face, and caught my flight back to Mexico City.

Andres was at my apartment when I arrived. "I need a hug," I said, before I could say anything else. He held me without asking questions, just a steady presence when I needed it most.

Later that day Dr. Peña and his wife came to check on me. He examined my face under bright light, gave me injections to prevent inflammation, and brought soup and fresh fruit his wife had prepared that morning. Their kindness undid me in ways the violence had not. I cried for the first time since waking up in Guadalajara.

Before I had seen the blood in the mirror, before I understood what had been taken, one thought had already arrived with absolute clarity in those first confused moments of waking.

I did not want to die this way. Not here. Not alone. Not like this.

Miami

I booked a flight to Miami for Monday morning. I needed medical care and familiarity and people who knew me before the hustle and noise, before Mexico City and warrior mode and all the ways I had been trying to prove I still mattered.

Andres took me to the airport early, paid for the taxi when I realized I did not have enough cash, and bought me breakfast at a café near the terminal. His care was steady and quiet, asking nothing in return.

In Miami my friend Lee picked me up at the airport and drove me straight to the Apple Store. I bought a new phone and waited as my Apple ID restored my messages, contacts, and threads of connection I had been chasing for months. Everything came back except what actually mattered.

I spent the week rebuilding what had been taken—new laptop, new phone, new wallet, replacement credit cards. I talked to my bank. I reset passwords. I moved through the practical tasks of recovery while avoiding the harder work of understanding what had actually happened.

I did not yet understand what else I had lost.

Just for today, I will not drink, smoke, use Xanax or poppers with you.

Thank you, God, for another opportunity to live another day.

I move onward and forward in Your grace.

I love you, Michael and Mike.

LESSON: GUADALAJARA

Guadalajara collapsed every story I had been telling myself about who I was and how I was living. Through the shock and fear and shame, one truth stood above the rest and would not be ignored.

I had replaced alcohol with work and work with validation and validation with sex. The substance had changed, but the hunger had not.

I had believed this pattern was harmless, even liberating in some ways. That I was living authentically, meeting my needs, staying sober while still having a life. That night made it impossible to ignore that it was neither harmless nor liberating. Not only because of the violence that can arrive suddenly when you put yourself in vulnerable situations with strangers, but because of the quieter damage that unfolds over time—the way this pattern keeps you from building something real while convincing you that intensity is enough, that being wanted is the same as being loved.

This was not about morality or judgment. It was about honesty.

Another layer of the warrior fell away that night in Guadalajara, not because I felt prepared to let him go or because I had learned the wizard's way of living, but because staying in that way of being would have killed me eventually, whether suddenly in a hotel room or slowly through isolation and emptiness.

Letting him rest was no longer philosophical or aspirational.

It was survival.

CHAPTER TWELVE: THE UNRAVELING

When I flew back to Mexico City in early April 2025, the jacarandas had exploded while I was gone. Purple petals scattered across sidewalks and filled the gutters, trees lit like small celebrations everywhere I looked. The city moved the way it always does, indifferent to individual trauma. I moved more slowly.

Andres began making our midday meals again—chicken or pork with salad, always plated neatly, always enough for two. Ordinary food that felt like care. I walked every morning, three miles at first, then five, then ten split across the day. I walked to the park, Reforma and Condesa. I tracked the distance not to win anything but to prove to myself that I was still here, still moving, still capable of putting one foot in front of the other.

The routine did not erase the trauma, but it made space for it to settle.

Processing

I called Kelly in late April and we talked for more than an hour. She had been researching Spain too, she told me, and it sat ahead of Italy and Mexico on her list of places she wanted to live. We talked about Guadalajara. She kept returning to one thing, gently but firmly: If Uchi had not been there, there would have been no help at all.

She was right. There had been no police, no ambulance, no concern from the hotel staff. The city had kept moving. I had been left to survive myself.

I called my mother in Arizona. She was struggling in the way ninety-two-year-olds struggle, still trying to make sense of what comes next while her body betrays her a little more each day. I could not fix it. I could only listen.

That night I wrote in my journal that Plan B was Spain, and by the next page I knew that Plan B was already becoming Plan A. Santiago made sense in a way that did not require defense. I could be close to the Camino, close to the rhythm that makes me human. I could walk when I needed to walk. I could tell stories about the path. Maybe even become a Gay Camino champion, whatever that meant.

Some afternoons I was okay. Some nights I was not.

Easter came in late April and with it the replays intensified. I woke groggy and disoriented, dreams thick with chemical residue. Sometimes I was being drugged again. Sometimes set up to be killed. The loop continued until I got out of bed and reached for the old escape hatch—pleasure to fight fear, control to replace chaos. I did not yet have the words, but I was trying to process trauma by recreating it.

I had underestimated trauma in ways I did not yet understand. I believed that by this point in my life, at sixty-three years old with decades of survival already behind me, I had already paid whatever price was required. Instead, the impact arrived quietly and then all at once. Nightmares pulled me out of sleep, and with them came an urge I could not explain at the time—a need to return to what had happened and somehow change the ending, to regain control over something that had stripped it from me.

What looked, from the outside, like relapse was my body trying to process what my mind had not yet caught up to. Trauma does not care how old you are or how much you have already survived. It lives in the body, and it speaks whether you are ready to listen or not.

I learned that recovery does not move in straight lines. It curves, doubles back, and spirals forward in ways that can feel disorienting if you expect progress to behave politely. I wrote the mantra and meant it. I broke it and meant it again. That rhythm was not a failure. It was part of the work, the slow and imperfect process of learning how to stay present when the body wants to flee.

Waiting for Rescue

For a long time I had been waiting for rescue, though I would not have named it that way. I waited for deals to land, for geography to solve what I could not face, for discipline or willpower to carry me through. None of it came, because it could not.

What I needed was not saving. It was honesty.

Leaving Mexico was not an escape. It was surrender. It was the quiet admission that I needed a different environment, closer proximity to what steadied me, and enough space to recover without performing recovery for anyone else.

By late April everything felt suspended. Work circled without landing—Pinto went silent, Septo Música stopped responding, others faded into vague promises. Relationships softened or drifted. Andres and I settled into something gentler and more distant, roommates who had once been lovers now becoming friendly strangers.

I began asking myself one question each day, not to fix anything but to orient myself: How am I going to show up as a first-class human and not a victim today?

The answers were small and imperfect, but they accumulated. Focus on my own life. Be available to those who respect me. I had to listen fully, speak clearly, and set boundaries without apology.

By May I was no longer walking for exercise. I was training up to ten miles a day. I was hitting the gym several times a week and eating simple food.

The Andres Pattern

Andres and I did not drift gently from lovers into something quieter. It happened the way my patterns usually happen, through urgency disguised as necessity.

When the hustle returned and my days filled with projects that needed follow-through, I converted intimacy into utility without admitting that was what I was doing. I told myself I was offering him opportunity, income, a role in something that mattered. What I was really doing was hijacking his life to meet whatever need in me was loudest at the moment.

When I needed connection, he was my lover. When I needed execution, he became my assistant. I blurred the line completely and then pretended not to notice the damage accumulating. He was not very good at being either, and that was my responsibility too. I had turned a relationship into a transaction, presence into productivity, and wondered why neither of us felt steady or whole.

The fault line was not subtle. I just kept stepping over it.

By the time Spain began to take shape in my mind as something real, we both understood what had happened even if we never named it aloud. When I gave him what remained in the apartment—furniture, kitchen things, the small comforts of a life being packed down—it was not severance and it was not generosity. It was an acknowledgment. I had taken more than I had any right to take, not through cruelty but through entitlement masquerading as care.

He deserved someone who wanted him, not someone who kept reshaping him to fill whatever gap felt most urgent that week. And I needed to face something I had avoided for a long time: The pattern that led to Guadalajara had not ended there. It had simply changed form, trading danger for control, chaos for productivity, but still using other people as solutions to problems I had not yet learned to sit with on my own.

I booked a flight for July. I packed the scallop shell, the yellow arrow stone, the pine cone from Galicia. I said goodbye to the few people who mattered without explaining where I was going or why, because I did not yet have words for what I was doing.

I only knew I needed to be closer to the Camino, closer to the thing that had shown me who I could become before I forgot again.

Madrid

When I boarded the overnight flight to Madrid on July 19, 2025, I slept fitfully and woke as the plane began its descent over Spain. The air that met me when I stepped outside the terminal was warm and almost tender, the kind of heat that feels like a welcome rather than assault.

The city opened around me without demanding explanation. Cafés spilled onto sidewalks. Voices rose and fell with the rhythm of the day. Strangers passed without needing anything from me.

After everything—after Guadalajara, after the unraveling, after watching every deal I had chased dissolve into silence—Madrid did not ask me to justify why I had come.

It simply said *bienvenido*.

And for the first time in a long while, I believed I was allowed to step inside.

For a few days, the city held me gently. Then the temperature rose and stayed there, pressing down with a relentlessness that turned beauty into endurance. One hundred and three degrees every afternoon. The streets shimmered. Cafés still spilled onto sidewalks anyway, voices lifting and falling with the day, the smell of espresso and sunscreen lingering in the air. Madrid was alive and confident and unapologetically itself, even when it became too hot to fully inhabit.

The first apartment I rented promised air conditioning. What it delivered was a cooling floor system that never cooled anything. Nights were sleepless, my body already raw from months of recovery, my nerves too exposed to negotiate discomfort. I spent hours on support calls, switching clumsily between Spanish and frustration, until they finally moved me to a small studio with real air conditioning. When sleep returned, so did a measure of sanity.

I built a rhythm before I built a life.

I walked early, before the heat took over, six miles through neighborhoods I barely knew. I learned where to buy groceries cheaply and where to spend a little more when comfort mattered. I found a gym with a pool and let the water steady me. On Monday afternoons, I went to English-speaking AA meetings, where familiar voices reminded me why I was still alive and what staying that way required. Each morning began the same way, with the mantra that had carried me this far, spoken quietly but with intention.

Work hovered at the edges of my days, close enough to feel but never solid. Pinto remained a possibility, filled with hopeful conversations and unclear timelines. Pinnacle lingered in promise. I wrote the proposal, named my rate, and sent it without apology or discount. Studio Sende continued to take shape slowly, thoughtfully, without urgency. Gladys Palmera, one of the most iconic brands in Latin music, remained beautiful and complex, and I knew exactly what it would take to unlock its value. I also knew I was no longer willing to chase it.

I posted on LinkedIn, more out of habit than strategy, and one post traveled farther than I expected. Thousands of views. Old names resurfacing. Messages arrived from people who still remembered my voice. The world was still listening. But I was not running toward it anymore. I was standing still long enough to see what might come on its own.

In my journal, I drew a line beneath a date. August 20, 2025. If nothing had landed by then, I would walk again.

The heat did not break. Days blurred into one another, shaped by long morning walks, slow afternoons, gym sessions, writing, and waiting. Madrid was cultured and grand and steady in its identity. But something else was pulling at me. I needed a horizon. I needed the sea. Portugal began whispering quietly, with its ocean air and slower pulse. Porto entered my thoughts more than once. Peace began to look like water and wind.

Loneliness softened during these times. It was no longer the hollow ache of Guadalajara, but a quieter presence, something like background noise. I was alone in a new city without community yet, tethered only by routine and a handful of people who truly knew me. I spent too much time scrolling on Grindr, not to meet anyone, but to reassure myself that I still existed in the world. Beneath that impulse, though, something else was stirring: a strange and terrifying freedom. I was unbound, had no apartment to protect and no company to represent. No expectations to manage except my own.

I stayed close to the people who mattered. I called my mother often, ninety-two years old and still sharp, our conversations circling small practical things that carried the weight of love. I called David and Tom and Kelly, anchoring myself to voices that knew my heart without explanation.

August 20 arrived without ceremony. No work had landed. Pinnacle had gone quiet. Iconic was still evaluating and Studio Sende remained interested but not yet ready. And instead of panic, I felt relief, because somewhere deeper than thought, I had already decided.

The Camino was calling again. Not as an escape or failure but as the logical next step.

What I had not yet said out loud, even to myself, was what I needed this walk to do. The first Camino had shown me that another way of being existed beneath the armor I had worn my entire life. This one was asking something more difficult and more final. It was asking me to take the armor off and leave it behind.

For sixty-three years, the warrior had kept me alive. He carried me through foster care, through coming out, through building and losing Fania, through addiction and sobriety and survival in every form that required vigilance and grit. He had done his job. But if I stayed in that mode, striving, proving, controlling, forcing, I would die. Maybe suddenly, the way Guadalajara had nearly ended me. Or maybe slowly, unable to imagine a version of myself that was enough without producing.

I did not need to destroy the warrior or pretend he had never served me. I needed to let him rest. To consciously stand him down. To stop asking him to solve problems that no longer belonged to him.

I did not yet have clean language for this realization. What I had was a knowing that lived deeper than strategy or ambition. Something in my life needed to change at the level of identity, not behavior. And the only place I had ever heard that kind of truth clearly was on the path.

I booked the train to Pamplona for August 24. From there, a bus to Saint-Jean-Pied-de-Port, France.

The heat finally broke on August 22, mornings turning cool, afternoons manageable. Still, I knew Madrid was a chapter at this point. When the train pulled out of the station, the city receded in soft gold light. Pamplona greeted me with cooler air, northern calm, and the familiar proximity of mountains and paths. I dropped my bag, wandered plazas, ate pinchos, and felt my breath even out.

The night before the walk, I packed my bag and left it by the door.

Tomorrow morning, the bus to Saint-Jean-Pied-de-Port and the morning after, the first steps of Camino Two.

This time, I was not running. I was walking toward something unnamed but waiting.

And this time I was starting in Saint-Jean-Pied-de-Port, France. Where the Camino Francés actually begins, high in the Pyrenees mountains.

LESSON: MADRID

What Madrid gave me was not clarity about work or certainty about the future. What it gave me was surrender.

I arrived believing that if I just applied enough effort, something would land. That pressure, discipline, and persistence would eventually force a door open. That stopping would mean failure. This was the warrior speaking, the part of me that had always believed survival depended on motion, that worth was measured by output, and that rest had to be earned.

But the longer I stayed, the clearer it became that the warrior had reached the end of his usefulness. He had kept me alive when danger was real and constant. He had protected me when there was no one else to do so. But he could not lead me into the second half of my life without destroying me in the process.

What I needed was not another deal, another partnership, or another round of proof that I still mattered. What I needed was permission to stop chasing long enough to see clearly. To stop forcing outcomes. To stop performing progress. To let go of the belief that my value depended on how hard I pushed.

I needed to let the warrior rest.

Not abandon him, erase him, or deny what he had done for me. But consciously set him down. Acknowledge that his vigilance, his urgency, his constant drive to prove had become dangerous. Guadalajara had shown me how close that path came to ending my life. Paul had shown me where it led if you could never stop. Madrid showed me that continuing in that way would be a slower version of the same ending.

Listening is not giving up. Choosing rest is not quitting. Drawing a line in my journal and honoring it was not a weakness, it was clarity. It was choosing the one path that had ever helped me meet myself honestly over the one that kept promising answers and never delivering them.

The second Camino was not about discovering who I was. I already knew. It was about learning how to live without armor. About trusting that I did not need to be on guard to be safe, or productive to be worthy, or impressive to be loved.

The Camino does not require certainty or confidence. It does not ask you to know where you are headed or who you will become along the way. It only asks that you show up and walk. Sometimes the bravest act is not pushing harder, but stopping long enough to trust that the walking itself will reveal what comes next.

Just for today, I will not drink, smoke, use Xanax or poppers with you.

Thank you, God, for another opportunity to live another day.

I move onward and forward in Your grace.

I love you, Michael and Mike.

PART THREE

THE RETURN

CHAPTER THIRTEEN: CROSSINGS

In August 2025, I returned to the Camino. The climb over the Pyrenees from Saint-Jean-Pied-de-Port was hard and incredible in the way only first days can be, when the body remembers something the mind has not yet caught up to. I left before sunrise on August 25, with George Winston's *Autumn* playing softly in my headphones, the same music I had listened to on my first Camino three years earlier, as if returning to a conversation that had never really ended.

The air was cool and still. The mist was thick enough to blur distance, and clouds drifted across my face like breath, dissolving the world into white. Cowbells rang somewhere ahead of me in the fog, steady and reassuring, guiding me forward through landscape I could not see. The path climbed relentlessly, switchback after switchback, my legs burning, my lungs working hard in the thin mountain air. My heart found its rhythm.

Up there, between France and Spain, it felt like walking inside something sacred. The mountains rose around me with a calm authority, ancient and unmoved by effort or ambition. The light shifted constantly, shadow giving way to gold and then back again, and as demanding as the climb was, it felt strangely nurturing, as though the landscape itself were holding me.

By midday I was deep in the clouds, walking without any view of where I had been or where I was going. There was only the path beneath my feet, the sound of cowbells, and the quiet trust that if I kept walking, I would arrive where I needed to be. I loved being back on the Camino, not because it was familiar, but because it asked me for nothing beyond presence.

The Camino Family

Somewhere between Roncesvalles and Zubiri, tucked away in the Pyrenees mountains in northern Spain, the Camino family began to form the way it always does—slowly, through repeated encounters that accumulate into something like friendship. At first I walked alone, keeping my own pace and rhythm, the music still in my ears. But the same faces appeared again and again at rest stops and cafés along the route. A nod turned into a greeting, a greeting into conversation, and before long we were walking together even when we were apart, that loose and generous kind of connection the Camino offers, where each person walks their own story while somehow becoming part of yours.

Neill from Ireland, tall and steady with an easy laugh. Merel from the Netherlands, organized and kind in quiet ways. Lynn from Taiwan. Lisa and Margie from the United States. Eric from Hong Kong. Toby from the Netherlands. Carlos from Costa Rica. Adrian from Scotland, younger than most of us, funny and bright but carrying something underneath the humor that I could sense but not name. I was surprised at how much younger the pilgrims were in this Camino.

Carlos and I walked side by side for several days between Pamplona and Logroño. He told me about his work building an intergenerational community in Santa Teresa, Costa Rica, a place where people of different ages could live and create together without the isolation that defines so much of modern life. He spoke with clarity and conviction, painting a picture I could see clearly as he talked. When he invited me to visit, I said yes without hesitation, trusting the feeling rather than worrying about logistics.

In Pamplona, I met Jose from Camino People for coffee in the plaza where sunlight warmed the stone beneath our chairs. We talked about pilgrims and purpose and the work I felt called to do with Camino Más Allá. I told him about my vision of coaching people before, during, and after the Camino, helping them walk not just the miles but the meaning, the transformation that happens when you stop performing and start being present. It was not a pitch or a business proposal. It was a conversation rooted in shared values. We agreed that collaboration mattered more than competition, and as I continued walking, I shared the idea with other pilgrims. Each time, something clicked. One woman from Australia said quietly that I was already doing the work simply by being there, listening, and holding space.

By the time I reached Logroño, my body had settled fully into the rhythm of the walk—early mornings, long days, simple meals, and deep sleep. My spirit had settled too, into a sense of peace I had not felt in a long time, maybe ever.

The Dinner

That night I hosted a Camino family dinner in the three-bedroom apartment I had rented in Logroño. It was larger than I needed for myself, with a long wooden table and windows that opened onto the street below where evening light turned the buildings gold. Merel helped organize the invitations and the space, moving through the room with quiet care. Neill and Adrian stayed with me in the extra bedrooms.

Everyone brought something to contribute. Carlos arrived first and took over the kitchen, cooking pasta with the easy authority of someone who feeds people as an expression of love. Neill brought cheesecake from a bakery he had discovered that afternoon. Bottles of wine were opened and passed around the table, though I stayed with water, and no one commented or asked questions.

The room filled slowly with pilgrims from eight different countries. Conversations layered over one another, laughter rising and falling, stories unfolding without urgency or agenda. Someone asked me to play music from my Fania days, and I pulled up one of the playlists I had made in Zipolite, songs that had shaped me at different moments across six decades. The music moved through the room, carrying memory and movement together.

What I remember most clearly is not what was said, but the quality of the presence. No one was performing. No one was trying to impress or prove anything. We were simply there, tired from walking, grateful for food and company, letting the evening unfold without direction.

Near the end of the night, Merel gathered everyone's attention and handed me a stack of folded pages. I did not understand at first. I assumed they were jokes or Camino traditions I had not yet learned. But when I looked around the table, their faces were quiet and serious, the kind of expression people wear when they are offering something that matters.

Someone told me to read them later, when I was alone.

I placed them carefully beside my journal without opening them, feeling the weight of something I could not yet name.

The Train to Madrid

The next morning, I got up early and had coffee with Adrian before he left to begin another day on the camino. I had a rest day. Before long Carlos was texting me that he had forgotten his coat. I told him not to worry, that I would send it with Adrian.

Adrian left early that morning to continue walking. I handed him Carlos's jacket as he stood in the doorway, asking him to return it when they met in Nájera. As he walked away down the street, I felt something I couldn't name—a hesitation, a sense that something wasn't right. I didn't know what to do with that feeling, so I ignored it

Merel was having foot problems and decided to stay an extra day and have it looked at. I invited her to stay with me in one of the extra rooms. We had an incredible day together and she had her foot seen by a doctor.

The next morning, I got up and caught an early train back to Madrid to catch a flight to Porto. I would spend a week checking out Porto, along the coast in Portugal, before starting the Camino Portugués up the coast and into Spain before turning inward to Santiago de Compostela.

As the countryside slipped past the window—vineyards and fields dissolving into one another, the landscape opening as we moved south—I reached into my pack and unfolded the notes.

Each one was handwritten. Each one was personal. And each one reflected back something I had not known I was showing.

They thanked me for being present, for listening without needing to fix anything, for creating space without needing anything in return. They spoke of calm, of steadiness, of a quiet strength that did not demand attention or validation. None of them mentioned achievement or endurance or how many miles I had walked. They were seeing me, not the warrior who had survived everything, not the hustler who closed deals, but the person I was when I stopped performing and simply showed up.

I read them slowly, one by one, as the train carried me south toward Madrid. Tears came before I could stop them, streaming down my face while the Spanish countryside blurred past the window. Something inside me softened, something that had been locked in place for a very long time.

Those notes did not simply thank me, they healed me. They were proof that connection could arrive without effort, that belonging did not require proving, that I could be valued for who I was rather than what I produced.

Somewhere between Logroño and Madrid, I understood what had happened the night before. The dinner had been the warrior's retirement dinner. I had not planned it or named it that way, but I had gathered witnesses and marked the end of a long service. The warrior who had carried me through foster care, through coming out, through building Fania and losing it, through addiction and sobriety and Mexico City and Guadalajara—he was being honored, not dismissed. Released, not rejected. His work was done.

Porto

From Madrid I flew to Porto, a city on Portugal's coast. The city opened around me with ocean air and expansive light that felt different from Madrid's intensity. I walked along the Douro River at sunset, cooked simple meals in the small apartment I had rented, and allowed life to arrive without force or agenda.

Work conversations hovered at the edges of my days without urgency. Studio Sende had a call scheduled. Iconic was still evaluating the Pinto proposal. Pinnacle had gone quiet. And for the first time, uncertainty did not undo me. I was no longer waiting for someone else to say yes so I could feel like I mattered. I already had my path.

The Atlantic stretched beyond my window, patient and wide and indifferent to my plans. I walked the city streets learning where things were. I went to the gym. I attended AA meetings in English. I prepared to walk again, not because I was running from anything, but because the Portuguese route from Porto to Santiago would complete what I had started.

On September 12, 2025, I would begin walking north along the coast. But for now, I rested in Porto, letting the ocean air clear whatever remained of the warrior's grip.

I packed my bag and wrote in my journal.

This time, I was not walking to survive. I was walking to live.

Just for today, I will not drink, smoke, use Xanax or poppers with you.

I love you, Michael and Mike.

In the grace of God, I move onward and forward.

LESSON: CROSSINGS

By the time I reached the second Camino, something in me had already come to an end, even though I did not yet have the language to explain it. I could feel the finality before I could name it. The life I had been living no longer fit, and continuing to move through the world the same way felt not only exhausting, but untrue.

After Guadalajara, after the trauma and isolation, and after every attempt to force myself back into motion through effort and control, the walking made something unmistakably clear. What was finished was not a career, a relationship, or a chapter. What was finished was the belief that survival was still the work. I no longer needed to live as though danger were always just ahead, or as though effort itself were proof of worth.

The second Camino did not bring a sudden revelation. It brought confirmation, quietly and repeatedly. Day after day, I was shown that I did not need to perform in order to belong. Connection arrived without strategy and community formed without effort. People met me where I was, not for what I could offer, but simply for my presence.

Retiring the warrior in Logroño was not a defeat but rather completion. I let him rest with gratitude, knowing that he had protected me long enough for me to choose something else. What stepped forward was not passivity, but trust. Not retreat, but a different way of moving through the world.

The wizard did not replace the warrior. He made him unnecessary.

This was not a pause. It was not a rest. It was a crossing. And once crossed, there was no returning to a life that required armor in order to survive.

CHAPTER FOURTEEN: WALKING ALONE

The Portuguese coast was beautiful in the way things are beautiful when you are not yet ready to receive them.

I began walking north from Porto on September 12, following boardwalks that stretched for miles along the Atlantic. Wooden planks worn smooth beneath my trail runners. The sky was wide and blue, the sand pale and endless, the water green and restless as it broke against rocks shaped by centuries of persistence. It was the kind of landscape that should have felt like grace, like reward for everything I had walked through to get here. Instead, it felt like walking through someone else's postcard, admiring something from a distance without quite knowing how to step inside it.

I was alone in a way I had not expected.

Not the kind of solitude I had known on the Meseta during my first Camino, where quiet opened into something expansive and generous, where emptiness made room for processing grief and revelation. This was different, more closed, more isolating. The route was poorly marked compared to the francés, yellow arrows appearing sporadically or not at all. The towns felt subdued, almost vacant. The *albergues* and hotels were half empty. I passed only a handful of pilgrims each day, exchanging nods but rarely words. There were no shared meals forming naturally, no Camino family gathering around me, no sense of being carried by collective momentum the way I had been from Saint-Jean to Logroño. There was just the ocean, the road, and whatever I had brought with me.

Days began early, often before dawn, with coffee that was

unpredictable and often unavailable. I walked with the Atlantic on my left and farmland on my right, passing through villages that felt more like interruptions than destinations. Shops were closed when I needed them. Cafés had chairs stacked on tables. Streets were quiet except for the sound of my own footsteps echoing on cobblestone. At midday, I sometimes saw no one at all, just laundry hanging from windows and the distant sound of the ocean.

The language barrier added another layer of distance. People had told me it would not matter, that English or Spanish would be enough on the Portuguese Camino. It was not, or perhaps the distance I felt was not linguistic at all, but internal, the residue of a life spent explaining myself into belonging, performing my way into connection.

Trying to Work

I tried working deals from my phone as I walked. Pinnacle wanted a call about Latin market strategy. Studio Sende sent questions about the Innovation Center proposal. Iconic remained in evaluation mode around Pinto, asking for more time and more information. I took calls standing on boardwalks overlooking the Atlantic, typing emails on benches with the ocean stretching endlessly in front of me, trying to convince people of my value while the water reminded me I had nothing to prove.

At some point—maybe day three, maybe day four—standing with my phone pressed to my ear while someone explained why they needed more time to consider a proposal I had already revised twice, I stopped listening. Not out of rudeness, but because I could no longer pretend these conversations mattered more than the water moving in front of me. I realized I was trying to make things happen that did not want to happen, forcing alignment that did not exist, manufacturing enthusiasm for work that felt increasingly like performance rather than purpose.

So I stopped trying to force it. Not dramatically. I let calls go to voicemail. I left emails in draft. I put the phone back in my pocket and kept walking, choosing the ocean over the hustle.

Even sex had followed the same pattern, I realized. Hours spent on Grindr trying to talk someone into wanting me, scrolling through profiles as if the right combination of words might finally make me feel whole. I had confused attention with intimacy, availability with connection, intensity with aliveness. The ocean was offering something different in its steady rhythm. Arrival without pursuit. Presence without persuasion.

The Softening

By the third or fourth day, somewhere between Esponsende and Viana do Castelo, on the Portuguese coast, the solitude began to soften. What had first felt like loneliness began to feel like space—space to let the noise settle, space to notice what I had been chasing without ever asking why.

I had spent most of my life pursuing proof of worth through movement and achievement and connection and productivity. Deals that would prove I still mattered. Partnerships that would validate my relevance. Relationships that required convincing someone to want me. The Camino had tried to teach me this on the Meseta three years earlier, but I had forgotten it in Mexico City when the hustler returned and convinced me that survival required constant motion.

Walking along the Portuguese coast, the Camino answered me quietly and without judgment, the way it always does when you finally stop talking long enough to listen: You already matter. You do not have to prove it here.

One day was particularly hard—September 16, I think, though the days had begun to blur together. Seventeen miles, most of it inland, away from the water that had become my anchor. The path wound through farmland and small towns where markers were faded or missing entirely.

I got lost twice, ending up in a village with a single restaurant that had no kitchen and a hostel several kilometers outside town. Dinner was two small empanadas and a pastry. The room was cold, the bedding thin, and sleep came in fragments interrupted by dreams I could not remember when I woke.

The next morning, I got up and walked anyway, because that was what you did on the Camino. You got up and you walked.

Viana do Castelo

Viana do Castelo was the first place that felt inhabited again after days of ghost towns and empty streets. A real city with movement and texture and life. People in the streets. Cafés open with tables full. A river cutting through the center with boats along the docks. I spent the afternoon sitting with a proper coffee in a plaza, watching families and couples move through the space, feeling myself reenter the world rather than just pass through it like a shadow.

That night I spoke with David on the phone from my hotel room. He had sensed something was off in my messages and asked how the Camino was going.

"It isn't," I told him honestly. "But that doesn't mean it's wrong. It just means something different is being asked of me this time."

"What do you think that is?" he asked.

I paused before answering, looking out the window at the river below. "Stop chasing. Start creating."

The words surprised me as I said them, but they felt true in a way that went deeper than strategy or business plans. I was not walking away from my life. I was walking toward a way of living that did not require constant pursuit, constant proving, constant motion to feel like I had earned the right to exist.

The Ocean's Teaching

The closer I came to the Spanish border, the clearer it became. The ocean became my teacher over those days of solitude and silence. It did not chase the shore. It arrived, again and again, shaping stone through presence rather than force, through persistence that was patient rather than desperate.

That was the wizard. That was the life I was walking toward.

On September 20, I would cross into Spain at A Guarda and begin the final stretch to Santiago. But for now, I walked the Portuguese coast alone, learning how to be with myself when no one was watching, when no validation was coming, when the only proof of my worth was the fact that I kept showing up.

Just for today, I will not drink, smoke, use Xanax or poppers with you.

Thank you, God, for another opportunity to live another day.

I move onward and forward in Your grace.

I love you, Michael and Mike.

LESSON: WALKING ALONE

The Portuguese coast taught me how to live without the warrior in ways the Spanish Camino could not.

After the connection and affirmation of walking from Saint-Jean to Logroño, where a community formed around me and those handwritten notes reflected back a version of myself I was only beginning to recognize, the solitude of Portugal felt, at first, like absence. There was no community forming around me, no shared rituals to anchor the days, no reflections coming back to tell me who I was. What I came to understand was that this emptiness was not a loss or punishment. It was a necessary clearing.

I needed times without witnesses, without feedback, without an audience. I needed to practice being present without performance. I needed to learn how to stay with myself not only when something arrived to validate my existence, but also when nothing did, when the only company I had was my own thoughts and the sound of the ocean.

The question beneath everything finally rose to the surface without distraction or noise to drown it out: Could I be enough without proving it? Could my life be meaningful without constant motion toward the next thing, the next deal, the next person who might want me?

The answer did not come through insight or effort or revelation. It came through silence and repetition. Through walking when the day offered nothing remarkable. Through staying when old habits suggested escape. Through choosing the path over the phone, the ocean over the hustle, presence over productivity.

The Spanish Camino showed me that the warrior could rest. Portugal taught me how to live once he did.

The crossing into Spain, when it came, would become a ritual of release. I was letting go of chasing outcomes, forcing alignment, and believing that worth had to be earned through strain and suffering. I was welcoming a different way of moving through the world, one rooted in presence rather than pressure, in trust rather than control.

The wizard does not demand certainty before moving forward. He trusts rhythm. He knows that showing up with care and attention creates its own gravity, that the right things find you when you stop chasing them. He walks, and what belongs arrives.

CHAPTER FIFTEEN: CROSSING INTO SPAIN

I woke up just after seven in the small apartment in Caminha, the last town in Portugal before the river. The street below was quiet, the light gray and undecided, and the only coffee I had was instant, which I drank anyway while standing at the window, watching the morning arrive without enthusiasm. My bag was already packed beside the door. The luggage transfer company would come in an hour. Everything essential had been decided before I went to sleep the night before.

I was ready to leave Portugal.

Not because Portugal had failed me or disappointed me. The coastline had been beautiful, the towns kind in their quiet way, the days honest in their difficulty. But somewhere along the way over the past week of walking alone, Portugal had come to represent in my mind a season of effort without arrival, of chasing work that never quite landed, of trying to force belonging in places where it would not settle. In my mind, fairly or not, it had become the landscape of striving, of the warrior's last stand. And standing there with that terrible instant coffee in my hand, I made myself a quiet promise: I would leave all of that behind on the Portuguese shore so I could be open to what came next on the Spanish side.

Sixty-three years old. Nearly four years sober. Two hundred and fifty miles into my second Camino.

I was tired of trying to make things happen through force and will.

I grabbed my daypack and walked down toward the Minho River, expecting something official, some kind of dock or ticket booth or organized departure point. Instead, I found a sidewalk, a stretch of waterfront, and eventually a small handmade sign leaning against a lamppost that read in cheerful hand-painted letters: *Popeye's Ferry*.

That was it. That was the crossing point.

A woman stood nearby with a clipboard, scanning the street like she was waiting for someone specific. When she saw me approaching with my backpack her face lit up and she waved enthusiastically.

"*¡Peregrino!*" she called, walking toward me with open arms.

Before I could say anything or introduce myself, she wrapped me in a hug, full and unguarded, like we already knew each other, like I was returning home instead of leaving.

"I'm so happy you're here," she said in accented English, pulling back to look at me. "You're crossing today."

I laughed, caught off guard by her certainty and warmth. "Yes," I said. "I'm crossing."

Nearby, another woman stood with a professional camera, offering photos to pilgrims waiting for the boat. The ferry woman waved her over and asked if she could take our picture together. We stood by the river, both smiling, the wide gray water behind us, and the photographer captured the moment without asking for payment or explanation.

Then the ferry woman turned to me and said, "You need one for your Camino. Just you."

She gestured toward the water. I stepped closer to the river's edge, the current wide and calm in the early morning light. The photographer raised her camera again. I nodded, and as she took the photo, I felt something in my body soften in a way I had not expected. Not happiness exactly, but readiness. The kind that comes when you are moving toward something instead of running from it.

Later, when I looked at that picture, I could see it clearly in the way I was standing, in the way I held myself. I looked like someone who had stopped bracing for impact.

The Crossing

The boat was small, barely large enough for a handful of people. There were only three of us crossing that morning—me and two younger pilgrims I had not seen on the Portuguese route. The captain helped us aboard, and the ferry woman hugged each of us again before stepping back onto the dock and waving as we pulled away from the shore.

"*¡Buen Camino!*" she called, blowing us a kiss.

I sat on the wooden bench at the back of the boat with my pack at my feet and watched the Portuguese shoreline begin to recede. The Minho River was wide and steady, gray-green under the cloud cover, and the motion of the boat was gentle enough that it felt like being carried rather than transported across distance.

The entire crossing, I kept looking back at Portugal disappearing behind us, half-expecting to see something lift off me as the distance grew. As if striving or fear or desperation might have a visible form once they were finally released, like smoke rising from a fire that had finally burned itself out.

I thought about my first Camino three years earlier, and how that walk had taught me who I was beneath the noise and armor. It showed me my values, my tenderness, my capacity for faith. But it had not taught me how to stop running, how to stand still long enough to let life come to me instead of chasing it down.

Three years later in Mexico City, I had still been trying to outrun the same fears, still believing that effort alone could make me safe, that productivity could prove I deserved to exist.

The Portuguese shore disappeared into the distance. The Spanish shore rose ahead of us across the water.

This is it, I thought. This is where I leave it behind.

Ten minutes on a small boat. A lifetime between shores.

Landing

When we docked in A Guarda on the Spanish side, the captain helped us off one by one, extending his hand as we stepped from the rocking boat onto the solid dock. My foot touched Spanish soil and something released in my chest, sudden and undeniable, like a fist that had been clenched for years finally opening.

I had been to Spain before. I had lived in Madrid earlier that summer. None of that mattered at this moment. This crossing felt different because I had decided it was different, because I had made it a ritual of release instead of just another border crossing.

No more chasing work that did not want to land. No more forcing outcomes that would not come. No more trying to prove I deserved to be here through hustle and performance.

The relief came immediately, without effort or struggle. I stood on the dock for a moment, breathing deeply, feeling tears press at the edges of my eyes, not from sadness but from gratitude. The kind that arrives when you realize you have been holding your breath for years and have finally let it go.

I walked into the small town of A Guarda and found a café open despite the early hour. I ordered a café con leche and a tortilla española and laughed when they arrived at my table. The coffee was strong and real, not instant. The tortilla was thick and golden, still warm from the pan. I ate slowly, savoring each bite, noticing how ordinary goodness feels extraordinary when you are present for it instead of rushing past it toward the next thing.

This was what it felt like to stop running and simply arrive. Not dramatic. Not ecstatic. Just here, present, grateful for strong coffee and good food and a seat by the window watching Spanish morning unfold.

Walking into Spain

Later that day, walking along the Spanish coast with the Atlantic on my left and green mountains rising quietly on my right, I noticed how little space fear was taking up in my mind. For months after Guadalajara, every stranger had felt like a potential threat, every city like a trap waiting to close. Now, watching waves break against rock and hearing my trail runners on the path, that vigilance loosened its grip. Not gone entirely, but softer, less in charge of my movements.

I ate lunch in a small village at a plastic table under the sun. An older couple walking past wished me *Buen Camino.* I returned the greeting, and the exchange stayed with me longer than it should have for something so small and ordinary. It mattered because it was kind. Because it was ordinary. Because it reminded me that the world was not out to harm me, that most people were simply living their lives and wishing pilgrims well.

That night, in a quiet room overlooking the ocean in Oia on the western coast of Spain, I wrote in my journal about the crossing and the promise I had made on Popeye's Ferry. I knew I would need to remember it. I knew there would be days ahead when I would be tempted to forget, when the old voice would whisper that I needed to hustle harder, prove more, force outcomes into existence.

But that night, listening to the waves and watching the light fade over the Atlantic, I felt something I had not felt in a long time, maybe ever.

I felt safe.

Just for today, I will not drink, smoke, use Xanax or poppers with you.

I love you, Michael and Mike.

And I move onward and forward in the grace of God.

LESSON: CROSSING INTO SPAIN

Transformation sometimes requires more than intention or understanding, more than something you can think through or decide in isolation. It needs a ritual. It needs a physical act that gives the inner shift a body, a moment you can point to later and say: That was when something finally changed.

I could have stopped chasing while sitting in an apartment anywhere in the world, and I had tried to do exactly that more times than I can count. I wrote it in journals, promised it to myself in quiet moments, and said it out loud in the hope that repetition would make it real. None of it held, not because the desire was insincere, but because the decision had never been anchored in my body.

What held was the crossing itself.

Leaving Portugal on a small boat and watching one shoreline slowly recede while another rose ahead of me, I felt something shift before I could fully articulate it. When my foot touched Spanish soil, I made a promise in that precise moment to stop chasing, to stop forcing outcomes, and to stop trying to prove that I belonged in the world through effort alone.

The ritual gave the commitment weight in a way language never had. The physical act made the internal change real, not metaphorical or aspirational, but embodied. In the space of a short crossing, I moved between two ways of living that had been separated by years of struggle.

That crossing was not symbolic to me. It was actual. I left behind in Portugal a season defined by desperation, by manufacturing outcomes, by believing that if I just tried harder I would finally feel safe. I stepped into Spain without plans or defenses, carrying only a willingness to be open to what might come instead of forcing what never had.

The relief arrived quickly and without effort because my body understood what my mind had been trying to accept for months. The crossing made the decision believable in a way that thinking about it never could.

Ritual matters because it gives form to transformation and allows the nervous system to catch up with what the heart already knows. Sometimes you have to physically leave one place and enter another before change can settle, breathe, and finally stand on its own.

CHAPTER SIXTEEN: VIGO—FALLING IN LOVE AGAIN

After A Guarda, the days along the western Spanish coastline began to blur together. I spent a night in Oia, then walked on to Baiona, the ocean staying close enough to shape everything without always being visible. Sometimes it was right there beside the path, sometimes only suggested by salt in the air and the sound of wind moving through the hills. The stages were not difficult on paper, but my body was carrying the accumulation of nearly two hundred miles. Each morning I felt it more clearly.

I had crossed from Portugal into Spain on Popeye's Ferry several days earlier, making a quiet promise to myself on the boat to leave the chasing behind. At the time, I didn't know exactly what that would mean. I only knew I was tired of forcing movement, tired of treating endurance like virtue. From A Guarda onward, I let the Camino unfold without urgency, one coastal town at a time.

By the time I reached Baiona, I knew I could push myself to walk the full stage into Vigo the way the Camino app suggested. I also knew I didn't need to. Choosing to take an Uber for the final stretch felt less like quitting and more like listening. Permission, not in a dramatic way, but in a deeply practical one. Permission to honor a sixty-three-year-old body that had done exactly what I had asked of it for weeks. Permission to choose ease without turning it into failure.

As we drove toward Vigo, the city appeared gradually. First the harbor opened wide and calm, mountains rising across the bay. Then the buildings came into view—old stone mixed with modern glass, balconies with iron railings, narrow streets climbing into green hills. The driver dropped me near my apartment in the center of the city, and I stood on the sidewalk for a moment, letting it settle. The place felt solid and lived in, as if it had no need to impress me.

I unpacked, ate lunch at a nearby café, and allowed myself to stop. No planning, no tracking distances, no checking maps.

That afternoon, I noticed an old pattern stirring. In the past, a city arrival like this would have sent me straight into distraction—scrolling, chasing, confusing attention with connection. I opened Grindr, then stopped. What I actually needed wasn't validation or intensity. It was care.

I booked a massage.

When Javier arrived later with his table and oils, there was nothing charged or performative about it. He worked quietly and professionally, focusing on my shoulders, my lower back, my calves tight from days of hills. I closed my eyes and let myself receive what I had asked for, without turning it into anything else or asking it to carry more meaning than it needed to hold.

When he left an hour later, I felt grounded in a way that surprised me. I had met a need directly, without compulsion or shame, without extending the moment beyond its purpose. That clarity stayed with me as I went back outside and walked into the city as it came alive for the evening.

Down by the harbor, the space opened wide again. Boats rocked gently at their moorings. Ferries arrived and departed with quiet regularity, their wakes spreading across the water. The promenade, lined with palm trees, filled slowly as the sky turned orange, then purple, then deepened toward night. Behind me, the city climbed into green hills, music drifting faintly through the streets.

I stood there a long time, watching the light change. The fear that had followed me since Guadalajara wasn't gone entirely, but it had loosened enough for something else to enter—curiosity, possibility, the simple pleasure of standing still without scanning for danger.

With the breeze coming off the water and the mountains darkening across the bay, I realized this wasn't a fantasy born of exhaustion. It was a clear, quiet recognition. I could live here in Vigo. Not as an escape or a temporary solution, but as something real and possible.

The next morning was Sunday, my rest day on the Camino. I woke without an alarm for the first time in weeks. I made coffee and stood at the window, watching the city move at an unhurried pace below. Later, I returned to the harbor and sat on a bench near the sailboats, letting hours pass as families walked the promenade and ferries slipped in and out of the bay.

For the first time in a long while, I didn't ask anything of myself. No emails. No deals. No next steps. Just sitting, breathing, and allowing the days to stop running together.

At some point, I thought about the life I had been trying to outrun for so long—the hustle, the proving, the constant motion toward the next thing that might finally make me feel secure. And I looked up the cost of living in Vigo on my phone, not as an escape plan or a strategy, but as a quiet curiosity. I did not make a decision or build a plan around it. I simply noticed that imagining a future without forcing it into existence felt like progress, like something the wizard would do.

That night, I went to bed early, knowing I would walk again the next morning toward Pontevedra and eventually Santiago. But I was grateful for what Vigo had offered me in the meantime. It had not promised answers or transformation or a place to hide from difficulty.

It showed me what life could feel like when I stopped chasing it and let it arrive on its own terms.

Just for today, I will not drink, smoke, use Xanax or poppers with you.

I love you, Michael and Mike.

And I move onward and forward in the grace of God.

LESSON: VIGO

Vigo showed me that the wizard's way is not abstract or aspirational, but practical and grounded in honesty. I used a familiar tool there—professional touch given and received—something I had relied on for years in different contexts, but this time I used it without compulsion or escape. I met a need directly and allowed myself to move on without turning the moment into something it did not need to become.

That difference mattered more than I initially understood. For much of my life, I had used attention, intensity, and connection as ways to outrun discomfort or prove my worth. In Vigo, I did not need to disappear into the experience or stretch it beyond its purpose. Care was enough on its own, and learning to accept that quietly changed the way I related to myself and my needs.

When you stop forcing outcomes and begin responding to your needs with clarity rather than avoidance, something inside you softens. You become available to the place you are actually standing instead of constantly scanning for validation or rescue. The present moment stops feeling like something to endure and begins to feel like something you can inhabit.

Presence does not come from discipline or performance. It arrives when you stop negotiating with your worth long enough to notice what has been steady beneath you all along. Vigo taught me that living this way is possible, not through grand gestures or dramatic transformations, but through small, honest choices repeated with care.

That was what falling in love again meant here. Not with another person, and not with a fantasy of who I might become if I just tried harder. It meant falling in love with the life that was already waiting for me once I stopped chasing it, forcing it, and demanding it prove I was worthy of living it.

CHAPTER SEVENTEEN: THE LAST 100K

The mountains in Galicia smell like wet earth and pine, and the morning I climbed into them from Redondela, the air was cold enough that I could see my breath. I had left the ocean behind at Vigo, and now the world narrowed into trees, stone walls, and paths that rose and fell through forests so dense they felt almost black in the early light.

The casa rural I had stayed in the night before sat tucked into the hills several kilometers outside town, a solid stone building with outdoor tables under a canopy where Rose from Germany and a couple from Brazil and another from the Netherlands had sat talking as the afternoon cooled. The conversation had been easy and unguarded, the kind that happens when everyone has been walking for days and nobody needs to explain who they are or prove why they matter. It felt like Camino spirit returning, that quiet sense of shared presence I had lost somewhere back on the lonely Portuguese coast.

Now, climbing through trees that closed overhead like a cathedral, I understood what had been changing. I had spent weeks letting go without fully realizing it was happening. Letting go of drinking and pills had come years earlier in Miami. Letting go of the career I had built and the version of myself I had tried to hold together with momentum and sheer willpower was newer and more painful. Somewhere between the ocean and these mountains, the work had sharpened into something I could finally hold without resistance.

You are enough.

The Crowded Path

The trail was crowded now in the last hundred kilometers before Santiago, which meant pilgrims who had started just days earlier mixed in with those of us who had been walking for weeks or months. Groups with matching backpacks stopped to take photos at every marker. Couples laughed loudly as they passed. The energy was busier and less intimidating than it had been before, but I did not mind because I had figured something out, and that understanding traveled with me quietly, unaffected by the noise around me.

I had chased almost everything in my life. Jobs that looked right on paper but felt wrong in my body. Men who were not interested until I convinced them to be. Opportunities I forced into existence through pressure, persuasion, and the belief that if I just pushed harder, something would finally lock into place. Too often, when I did get what I had been chasing, I discovered that it no longer mattered, or that it had never been what I wanted in the first place.

The path climbed through the trees and opened briefly onto a ridge where the sky stretched clean and blue, clouds hanging over the hills as if they had been painted there deliberately. My legs knew what to do, one foot after the other, and the rhythm allowed my mind to move without panic through what I had been avoiding. I began to wonder what it would feel like to simply be present in my own life, to show up as myself and allow things to come rather than always going after them, to save my energy for what arrived naturally instead of burning it all trying to make something happen that was not ready or not right.

A young tour guide from Latvia walked beside me for a while that afternoon, talking about packs and routes and whether anyone really needed someone else to show them the way when the yellow arrows made it clear enough, even though he had done just that on the French route. After he peeled off at the next village, I stayed with my thoughts, returning again to the same patterns I had repeated for years around relationships and sex and the quiet fear of being alone.

I thought about the hours I had wasted trying to talk someone into wanting me, not because I desired them deeply, but because I wanted to feel chosen by someone, anyone. Even when something happened, I often left feeling more alone than when I started. I could not remember the last time intimacy had felt easy or mutual or unforced, the last time I had not been performing or convincing or chasing.

The trail dipped into a valley and climbed again, bodies crowding the narrow path until I found my pace and space opened back up around me. My dreams had been restless for days, full of arguments and handcuffs and familiar scenes of loss and control, my nervous system releasing things I could not consciously manage. All I could do was keep walking and trust the process of release.

I had called my mother from the casa rural that morning before leaving. Her voice sounded smaller than usual, though she was still sharp enough to know exactly what I was not saying. We talked around it, both of us aware of what was coming and neither of us naming it directly. Some truths do not need to be spoken to be understood.

The Playlist

The day I played my playlist, walking from Caldas de Reis toward Padrón. The sky was the kind of blue that only comes in fall when the air is clean and the light cuts sharply through the trees. I had been working through the list for days, eight hours of music that had carried me through different eras of my life, each song connected to a memory or a survival tactic or a version of myself I had once needed to be.

When Fania came on, something inside me slowed and went still.

I kept walking, but inwardly everything stopped moving.

The song was familiar, its brass and piano and voice cutting through the air in a way that stopped me mid-thought, and suddenly fifteen years collapsed into the space of a few steps on the trail. The call had come in 2006 from Robert, my business partner at the time, and an associate of his named James, about reviving a label that had once defined an entire movement before falling into neglect and legal chaos. The catalog was extraordinary, filled with voices and rhythms that had shaped generations, and I had said yes before he finished explaining what it would take.

What followed were some of the most meaningful years of my professional life. We cleared legal tangles that had paralyzed the catalog for decades, rebuilt the brand with intention and care, and brought the music back into the world where it belonged. I remember standing at Madison Square Garden watching thousands of people dance to the Fania All-Stars—grandparents who remembered the Palladium in the 1970s, parents who had grown up with the records, and kids discovering the music for the first time. The sound moved through them all, collapsing times and history into joy, and in those moments I knew the work mattered in ways that had nothing to do with charts or streaming numbers or quarterly reports.

I had the wonderful opportunity to relaunch this amazing brand over fifteen years. We remastered original albums, created box sets, vinyl reissues, remixed many of the songs, and worked with today's top artists on sampling many of the classics. We created club events in New York City, the original home of Fania, and brought the music and the brand to a new generation. We celebrate the label's fiftieth anniversary with fifty events one summer in New York, including several events at SummerStage in Central Park. In the end we had taken an old brand and label from a shed in the Hudson Valley and brought it back to life. Then the offers came and it was sold for a massive $35 million gain.

What I hadn't done was negotiate a fair equity position, and when it was sold I was given a small management payout, thanked for my years, and sent on my way.

I carried that bitterness into everything that came next. Every deal I chased afterward was an attempt to recover not money, but validation, proof that I mattered and that my work had value. All of them were variations on the same theme: If I could just close this one deal, if I could just prove myself one more time, then maybe I would finally feel secure.

The Release

Sitting there on the trail with the music moving through me and my trail runners planted on ancient stone, I finally understood what Fania had actually taught me. The work had been extraordinary because of what it gave to others, not because of what it gave back to me. The warrior needed Fania to prove his worth, to justify his existence, to silence the voice that said he was not enough. The wizard understood that the work itself was the point, that contribution mattered regardless of who received credit, that worth was inherent rather than earned.

I realized then that letting go did not mean regret or erasure. I was proud of what we built and of the care I brought to it through difficult years when others might have given up. What needed to change was not my relationship to the past, but my grip on the future. I could honor what had been without insisting it define what came next. I could carry the lessons forward without dragging the attachment behind me.

As the trail dropped into Padrón in the afternoon light, the tears came without warning. They were not sad tears. They were grateful tears. Grateful for my life, for the chance to stand here still walking, still open, still learning. With twenty-five kilometers left to Santiago, I could finally see the shape of the story I was living.

I am enough.

Not after the next job, not after the next relationship, not after proving something to someone who stopped paying attention years ago, but now, exactly as I am.

The path opened into rolling hills divided by stone walls that had stood for centuries, and I followed it with a quiet trust that felt unfamiliar but steady. One thought rose clearly and stayed with me for the rest of the walk: It is a privilege to be in my life, and that includes me and how I treat myself.

That night in Padrón, I showered, ate a simple meal, and went to bed early, ready for the final stage ahead. Tomorrow I would walk into Santiago. But the transformation had already happened here on these hills, listening to music that once defined my worth and finally understanding that my worth had never depended on it in the first place.

Just for today, I will not drink, smoke, use Xanax or poppers with you.

I love you, Michael and Mike.

And I move onward and forward in the grace of God.

LESSON: THE LAST 100K

Letting go, truly letting go, has been the hardest lesson of my life and also the one that finally set me free. Not the idea of letting go or the intellectual understanding of why it matters, but the lived act of releasing something I had been gripping for years because I believed it was the only thing keeping me safe.

I had said the words before, written them in journals, spoken them to friends, and carried them with me for hundreds of miles across Spain and Portugal. But none of that was the same as actually loosening my hold. There comes a moment when understanding stops being enough, when insight no longer moves the body, and when explanation gives way to action because the body finally releases what it has been guarding long after the mind has already moved on.

For me, that thing was Fania.

I had carried it into the future in my imagination for so long that I could not picture my life without it somewhere in the frame. It had been proof that I knew what I was doing, the story that made me legible and relevant in rooms that mattered to me, and letting go of it felt like stepping off a cliff without knowing what would rise to meet me.

What I learned was that letting go did not mean regret or shame. The work mattered. The culture mattered. What people experienced at those concerts and through that music mattered deeply and always will. What had to change was my grip on needing Fania to secure my future or define my worth as a human being.

Somewhere between the Atlantic and the mountains of Galicia, that fear softened into something steadier than reassurance, and I began to understand, not as a concept but as a lived truth, that I was already enough exactly as I was. Letting go of Fania did not mean abandoning music or the work that shaped me. It meant releasing the need to anchor my identity to a single chapter of my life, trusting that I could carry the lessons forward without dragging the attachment behind me.

Holding on had kept me standing still, chasing validation through deals that would never close. Carrying the lessons allowed me to walk again, free from the need to prove anything to anyone.

The Camino taught me that letting go is not passive and it is not clean. It often involves tears, long miles, and quiet rituals that finally give the body permission to release what the heart already knows. What matters is not how you let go, but that you actually do it, because until you release what you are clinging to, you cannot be open to what is waiting to meet you next.

CHAPTER EIGHTEEN: SANTIAGO—I AM ENOUGH

The tears came as I left Padrón the next morning.

They were not heavy or dramatic, not the kind that stops you mid-step. Just a few that slipped down my face as I walked away from the hotel in the early morning light, my pack settling onto my shoulders in the familiar way it had learned over weeks of carrying it. Twenty-five kilometers remained to Santiago, the final stage of my second Camino.

I was not crying for what was ending. I was crying for what I had gained.

The path opened ahead of me, quiet and empty in the predawn darkness. No pilgrims in sight, just cool air and the sound of my trail runners on stone. For the first stretch, I walked completely alone, and it felt right, like this was how the final day needed to begin.

Three years earlier, on my first Camino, I had walked into Santiago with Daniel and Liam beside me. I had needed witnesses then, needed companionship and confirmation, the shared recognition that something meaningful was happening. This time was different. I did not need anyone to validate my arrival. I could walk this last stretch alone and know exactly what I had done and why it mattered.

The solitude was not loneliness. It was completion!

The Final Walk

As the sun climbed, my body found its rhythm without effort. The heaviness I had carried for days lifted, replaced by a quiet steadiness that felt earned rather than forced. Overhead, the grape canopy appeared again, vines heavy with fruit, the leaves filtering light across the path in shifting patterns. I had walked under these grapes for days through Galicia, and now they accompanied me one last time, like a benediction offered without ceremony.

I walked the entire twenty-five kilometers alone that day. I stopped only when I needed water or a bathroom, otherwise letting forward motion carry me without interruption. One foot, then the other. The path beneath me and Santiago ahead.

By mid-morning, I put in my earbuds and returned to the playlist I had been walking with for days, the top one hundred songs that had carried me mile after mile. Memory followed memory, not pulling me backward, just passing through as the music played.

Just before the outskirts of Santiago, I stopped beneath a small bridge where a local man was offering special waxed stamps for pilgrim credentials. I pulled out my earbuds to ask for one, and that is when I heard it: salsa music echoing off the stone walls.

I looked down at my phone. Fania was playing in my ears.

The coincidence stopped me in place. Salsa in the real world, Fania in my headphones, the past and present meeting under a bridge just outside Santiago. Something in my chest loosened and settled.

I had a great run with Fania. Some of the hardest years in the music business, and work I was deeply proud of. I had helped bring something back to life that mattered to people across generations and borders.

But it could not define me for the rest of my life.

Standing there, I thanked myself for the care I had brought to that work, for showing up through years that demanded everything I had. And then, quietly and without drama, I said the word out loud: "Next."

It felt clean, like closing a door that had stayed open long after it needed to be shut. I pressed the stamp into my credential and kept walking toward Santiago.

A few minutes later, my phone buzzed with an email. Jose, with the reply I had been waiting for about working together on Camino tours the following year. He liked the details and felt it aligned with his brand. Asked for a week to review everything and suggested reconnecting after that.

I smiled and put the phone away. I did not need to chase it or force an answer. Whatever was coming would arrive in its own time.

The Plaza

The approach to Santiago looked different from my first Camino. We entered from another direction, the streets unfamiliar until, suddenly, my body recognized the place before my mind did. The plaza opened in front of me, wide and bright, the cathedral rising golden against the afternoon sky.

I stood there for a moment, taking it in without needing to perform emotion or manufacture meaning. I asked a passerby to take a photo, then offered to take one with him. We stood side by side in front of the cathedral, two strangers without a shared language, both smiling for the same reason because we both knew where we were and what it meant to have walked here.

Inside the Pilgrims' Office, the line moved slowly with hundreds of pilgrims waiting for their certificates. When my turn came, the woman behind the counter asked if I wanted both versions, the Latin Compostela and the detailed English certificate. I said yes. She leaned forward slightly as she handed them to me and said gently, "It's the journey you take from this experience, not the paper."

I bought both anyway, smiling at the truth she had offered.

The Cathedral

The next morning, I entered the cathedral and found a pew near the back, where light filtered through the high windows and fell in long beams across the stone floor. I sat and waited, not sure what I was waiting for but trusting that I would know when it arrived.

Three years earlier, I had sat in this same cathedral newly sober, newly sixty, still learning how to live without the numbing I had relied on for decades. That first time, the space had felt vast and overwhelming, and I had cried without fully understanding why.

This time, the space felt quieter, smaller even. Not because the cathedral had changed, but because I had.

I was not looking for forgiveness or proof or reassurance that I was on the right path. I already had those things. What I felt instead was something simpler and more complete—peace. Not the kind that arrives suddenly or announces itself with trumpets and revelation, but the kind that grows steadily beneath everything else until you finally notice it has been there all along.

I did not need the cathedral to tell me I was enough. I already knew.

But sitting there, I let that knowledge deepen, letting it move from my head into my chest and my bones, where it could live without explanation or defense. For years, I had believed that life would finally begin after the next accomplishment, the next chapter, the next proof that I mattered. Sitting there in the cathedral, I could see clearly that life had been asking something else of me all along—not achievement, not validation, just presence.

Leaving Santiago

When it was time to leave Santiago the next day, the rain returned in full force. No taxis came despite repeated calls to three different companies. I grabbed my suitcase and walked the twenty-five minutes to the train station in the downpour, rain soaking through my jacket, water running down my face, my shoes squelching with every step.

I laughed out loud walking through the streets. If I could walk hundreds of miles across Portugal and Spain, I could certainly walk twenty minutes in the rain to catch a train.

As the station came into view through the downpour, I felt clear about one thing. I did not know what came next in my life. But I knew how I intended to live.

I was done chasing what would not come. I was done forcing outcomes that were not ready. I was done trying to prove I was worthy of a life I was already living.

The warrior's work was complete. What stepped forward in his place was not passivity or retreat, but trust. The wizard does not force outcomes or chase validation. He shows up with care and attention and allows what belongs to meet him in its own time.

I was finally ready to live that way.

Just for today, I will not drink, smoke, use Xanax or poppers with you.

I love you, Michael and Mike.

And I move onward and forward in the grace of God.

LESSON: SANTIAGO — I AM ENOUGH

For most of my life, I believed that worth was something I had to earn, prove, and defend. That if I stopped producing, stopped achieving, stopped demonstrating value, I would somehow cease to matter. This belief shaped everything—the way I worked, the way I loved, the way I moved through the world wearing armor I could never quite remove.

The warrior was built on that foundation. He survived by proving. He measured worth by output. He believed that rest had to be earned and that safety came from constant vigilance. For decades, that framework kept me alive. It got me through foster care, through coming out, through building a career from nothing, through addiction and early sobriety. The warrior served me brilliantly when survival was the work.

But somewhere along the way, survival stopped being the work, and the warrior did not know how to retire. He kept proving, kept chasing, kept forcing outcomes long after the danger had passed. The desperate deals that would not close. The relationships I tried to manufacture through convincing. All of it was the warrior trying to earn permission to exist again.

Santiago did not teach me I was enough. It revealed what had been true all along but buried beneath decades of striving.

I am enough. Not because of what I have accomplished or survived or built. Not because of Fania or the Camino or sobriety or any single chapter of my life. I am enough because worth is not earned. It is inherent. It exists before achievement and remains after failure. It cannot be added to or diminished. It simply is.

Self-respect is not given to us by others, and it is not discovered by accident on a pilgrimage or in a cathedral. It is built slowly, often quietly, through the promises we keep to ourselves when no one else is watching. It grows when we stop abandoning ourselves for approval and begin honoring our energy, our boundaries, and our truth. It deepens when we choose presence over performance, when we allow rest without earning it, when we trust that showing up as ourselves is already more than enough.

The second Camino did not give me this understanding as a gift or revelation. It gave me the space to finally stop running long enough to hear what had been trying to reach me for years. In the solitude of Portugal. In the ritual crossing into Spain. In Vigo, choosing care over compulsion. In the mountains of Galicia, releasing Fania. In every step toward Santiago, the message repeated itself until my body finally believed it: You are enough. You have always been enough. You will always be enough.

Once you know that—not intellectually, but in your bones—you stop chasing what was never meant to be caught. You stop forcing doors that will not open. You stop performing for approval you do not need. And you become available for the life that has been waiting patiently for you to arrive.

That is what Santiago gave me. Not a certificate or a stamp or proof of completion. It gave me permission to stop proving and start living.

And that, finally, was enough.

CHAPTER NINETEEN: AFTER THE CATHEDRAL

The Camino did not end when I stepped out of the cathedral in Santiago.

It loosened instead, gradually and without ceremony, the way something essential releases its grip only after it knows it has done its work. There was no single moment I could point to as an ending. The rain-dark streets, the walk to the train station, the train pulling away from the platform, the countryside sliding past the window—none of it carried the drama of arrival or departure. What I felt was an easing, a sense that the urgency I had carried for so many years was no longer required to keep me moving.

I watched Galicia recede through the train window, the green hills dissolving into mist, farms and villages appearing and disappearing in a gentle blur. The landscape softened as it passed, and something in me softened with it. I did not feel triumphant or resolved or finished. I felt quieter, more settled, as if the road had done its job and was now stepping back, trusting me to take it from here.

Returning to Logroño

Before returning to Madrid, in early October, I went back to Logroño. It was not planned with intention or longing. I had booked accommodations for the wrong month when I first arranged my Camino schedule and could not change the dates, and my first reaction was irritation at myself for the mistake. Old instincts surfaced immediately—the urge to correct, optimize, and move on efficiently. But the moment

I arrived in Logroño, I knew the timing was not wrong at all. It was generous in ways I could not have anticipated.

I stayed in the same apartment building where we had gathered weeks earlier for our Camino Family dinner, the place where laughter had filled the rooms and handwritten notes had passed across the table without anyone knowing how much they would later matter to me. Returning without the daily momentum of walking allowed everything to settle differently. There was no urgency, no itinerary, no sense of needing to move on quickly to the next stage.

Logroño in October was quieter, gentler, no longer charged with the heightened intimacy that comes from shared exhaustion and approaching endings. I walked the same streets slowly, not as a pilgrim passing through on the way to somewhere else, but as someone revisiting a place that had already given him something essential. I sat in cafés where we had eaten together. I walked past the apartment where we had cooked pasta and shared wine and music. I got together with Donna, a pilgrim I had met from my previous camino who was doing it again as well.

I reread the notes people had written me that night, not looking for reassurance or validation, but noticing how they now felt less like encouragement and more like recognition of something that was already true. They reminded me that healing had not arrived through effort or insight or revelation, but through presence. Through opening my door to others. Through allowing myself to be known without performing. Through trusting that connection did not have to be earned through usefulness or achievement.

Those few days in Logroño mattered more than I realized then, giving me space to let the Camino finish its work in my body before returning to ordinary life. And for the retirement to set in.

Madrid

When I returned to Madrid, the city met me differently and I met it differently too.

I was no longer arriving as a warrior scanning the horizon for opportunity, validation, or proof that I still mattered in rooms where deals got made. I arrived as a wizard, attentive and unhurried, grounded in what had already been lived rather than what still needed to be accomplished. The difference was subtle but unmistakable, and Madrid seemed to recognize it immediately.

I walked La Latina in the mornings, its narrow streets opening slowly as the city woke, cafés setting out chairs on cobblestones, shopkeepers greeting one another by name with easy familiarity. In Chueca, I felt a different energy—open, unapologetic, alive with the confidence of people who had already fought to exist and were now simply living without apology. I wandered through Malasaña and Chamberí without an agenda, letting the city introduce itself block by block, noticing how history and daily life coexisted without strain or performance.

There was beauty everywhere, but it did not ask to be consumed or Instagram-ed or turned into content. It invited participation instead, quiet presence. I noticed older men lingering for hours in the same cafés, respected not for what they were producing now, but for the lives they had already lived. Writers, artists, thinkers, elders moved through the city without urgency, recognized simply for being who they were rather than what they could deliver.

For the first time in my life, I felt what it meant to be invited rather than evaluated.

My days found a gentle rhythm without effort. Morning coffee on the balcony of my apartment. Journaling without an agenda or outcome. Walking not as training or preparation for the next thing, but simply because moving through the city felt good in my body. Over time, faces became familiar without needing formal introduction. The flower vendor near the corner nodded when I passed. The barista who no longer asked for my order. The quiet acknowledgments that signal you are no longer passing through but becoming part of the fabric.

I was becoming part of the rhythm instead of brushing against it.

The Meeting

On a Monday afternoon in early October, I walked into an AA meeting I had found online and immediately loved. There was nothing flashy about it, no performative wisdom or dramatic storytelling. Just people sitting in a circle in a community center, telling the truth about their lives with humility and humor, supporting each other through the daily work of staying sober.

When it was my turn to share, I spoke about the Camino, about walking, about what sobriety had made possible over the past four years. I did not perform or package my story for effect. I simply told the truth about where I had been and where I was now.

I was met with warmth, curiosity, and a depth of listening that surprised me. People came up to me after the meeting and asked if I needed help in moving back. They welcomed me back to next week's meeting before I had even left. I walked out of that room with the unmistakable sense that there was space for me there, not as a visitor or outsider, but as part of a community that understood exactly what it meant to rebuild a life one day at a time without guarantees or certainty.

Full

A few days after leaving Santiago, I texted Kelly something I had been feeling but had not yet found words for, for a second time: *I feel my soul is full again.*

It was true in a way I had not experienced since my first Camino three years earlier.

What surprised me more was something I had written in my journal that final morning in Santiago and only fully understood later when I reread it in Madrid: *It's almost like I met a new friend and I really like the person, but it is actually me being with me.*

For the first time in my life, I was not just tolerating my own company or filling silence with distractions. I was enjoying being with myself, finding pleasure in my own thoughts and rhythms without needing external validation or entertainment.

That shift changed everything.

Coming Home

For most of my adult life, whenever I felt anxious or depressed, I would say the same thing: I want to go home.

I said it in hotel rooms across the country. I said it in Mexico City apartments. I said it in Miami Beach, standing in my own kitchen. I said it even when I was already home, or at least in the physical place I called home.

For years, I thought something was wrong with me. That I was fundamentally restless, incapable of settling, always chasing some elusive feeling of safety that would arrive once I found the right city, the right apartment, the right relationship, the right job. The warrior in me believed that home was something to be earned through achievement, that I had to prove myself worthy of rest and belonging before I could finally feel safe.

I tried everything, I moved cities, changed careers, and redesigned my space. I dated, broke up, dated again. I convinced myself that the next change would finally bring the feeling I was searching for. But the ache never left. "I want to go home" became a refrain I carried everywhere, a persistent longing that no external change could satisfy.

What I understand now and what the second Camino finally taught me, is that I was never homesick for a place.

I was homesick for myself.

Home is not something you arrive at after enough miles or enough healing or enough transformation. It is not a destination you reach once you have proven yourself worthy. Home is the practice of being present in your own life, doing what you are meant to be doing, and taking care of yourself in this exact moment.

The Camino taught me to ask a different question.

When that old feeling surfaces now, the restlessness, the anxiety, the desire to be somewhere else—I no longer say "I want to go home." I ask instead: *What do I need right now to feel at home?*

Sometimes the answer is rest, sometimes it is movement, and sometimes it is calling someone I trust. Sometimes it is simply sitting still long enough to let my nervous system remember that I am safe, that I am cared for, that I am exactly where I need to be.

Home is not a reward for good behavior or proof of having arrived. It is the ongoing practice of checking in with yourself and responding with care instead of criticism. It is the practice of asking what you need and then allowing yourself to receive it without shame or justification.

That is what wizard mode makes possible. The warrior believes home must be earned, that safety comes from control, that rest is what you get after you have done enough. The wizard understands that home is not somewhere you go. It is something you practice, a way of being with yourself that does not require external validation or perfect circumstances.

On that bench in León three years earlier, when I looked at the Meseta and saw Globe, Arizona, and spoke those words—I move onward and forward in the grace of God, I felt for the first time that I knew who I was. That moment was real and necessary. But what I did not yet understand was that knowing who you are is not the same as feeling at home in your own skin. You can know yourself intellectually and still feel like a stranger in your own life.

The second Camino gave me the rest of it. Not just knowing who I am, but trusting how I move through the world. Not just recognizing myself, but enjoying my own company. Not just accepting where I am, but feeling genuinely at peace being here.

That is what coming home means. Not arrival, but presence. Not achievement, but practice. Not perfection, but care.

And for the first time in my life, when I wake up in Madrid or walk the streets of La Latina or sit in an AA meeting or open my journal in the morning, I do not feel the old longing to be somewhere else. I feel at home in my life, not because everything is resolved or certain but because I have learned how to be present with myself exactly as I am.

The Camino gave me that. Not as a gift or a revelation, but as a practice I learned by walking the same path twice, carrying different questions, arriving at different answers.

And now, wherever I am, I know how to come home.

Building vs. Proving

When conversations about work surfaced with old colleagues who reached out during my times in Madrid, I noticed myself responding differently than I would have even six months earlier. An old contact from the music industry asked what I was building next, assuming the familiar urgency and hustle would still be there driving me forward.

I told him the truth without apology or explanation. I was not chasing anything right now.

He laughed. "When did that happen?" he asked. "When did you stop being the person who always has three deals in motion?"

"When I learned the difference between building something that matters and building something that proves I matter," I replied.

The wizard does not chase opportunities. He recognizes the ones that belong and allows the rest to pass by without attachment or regret.

Madrid made space for that understanding. It honored what had already been done without asking for more. It welcomed contribution without demanding productivity as proof of worth. It invited sharing instead of striving, presence instead of performance.

The Beginning

That invitation is how this book began, not as a plan or a proposal or a strategy to prove my value, but as an offering. A way to give back what had been given to me. A way to name what happens when you stop chasing and start noticing. A way to honor the road, the people, and the quiet wisdom that emerges when the wizard finally steps forward and takes his place.

Madrid did not feel like a city I was passing through on my way to somewhere more important. It felt like a place where I belonged, where I could build a life that was mine rather than one designed to prove something to people who were no longer paying attention.

But I was not ready to stay yet. There were practical matters to handle—finances, logistics, the work of actually relocating a life across an ocean. I flew back to Miami with a clear intention: return to Spain in April 2026 to begin the life I had finally learned how to live.

The Camino had taught me how to walk. Madrid had taught me how to stand still without panic. And now, back in Miami with a plan that felt like trust rather than force, I would prepare for the next crossing.

But that was not the ending. It was just the next step.

Just for today, I will not drink, smoke, use Xanax or poppers with you.

I love you, Michael and Mike.

And I move onward and forward in the grace of God.

EPILOGUE: JUST FOR TODAY

One morning I was sitting in a friend's backyard in Miami, sunlight moving through the trees, when I got on a video call with Carlos. We were supposed to be talking about music, a project for one of his friends in Costa Rica, something that might turn into work. It was the kind of conversation that feels important until it quietly isn't.

Halfway through, Carlos stopped speaking. His face changed in a way I recognized immediately, the shift that happens when something heavier needs to be said.

"Do you remember that morning in Logroño," he asked carefully, "when Adrian left your apartment with my jacket?"

I did remember. And until that moment, I had no idea what happened after Adrian walked out my door.

The night before, we had shared a pilgrims' dinner at my apartment in early September. I had rented a place with extra rooms, and Adrian had stayed in one of them. Carlos had been there too, and sometime during the evening he had left his jacket behind on a chair. The next morning Adrian was leaving early to continue walking, and I handed him the jacket as he stood in the doorway, asking him to return it when they met again in Nájera.

As Adrian stood there with the jacket over his shoulder, I felt something I could not name. A hesitation in my body, a subtle sense that something was not right. I did not know what to do with that feeling, so I ignored it. I watched him walk away down the street.

Carlos took a breath and told me what happened next.

Adrian walked out of my apartment carrying the jacket. At some point that morning he stopped at a bar in a village along the route. He drank and then he kept walking until he reached a place where he left his backpack on the trail—passport, money, computer, everything that made his life traceable—and climbed up a mountain and jumped.

Later that day Carlos arrived in Nájera. His phone rang. It was a close friend from home, the kind who calls without explanation and whom you answer without hesitation.

"Have you been to any churches on your Camino?" the friend asked.

Carlos said he had not.

"You should," the friend replied without explaining why.

Carlos found a monastery a few hundred meters away and walked inside. He did not try to explain what happened there when he told me the story, only that something shifted inside him. When he left and went to the municipal albergue to check in, the manager overheard him asking other pilgrims about Adrian.

"Two women found a backpack on the trail," the man said. "Money, passport, computer. They're trying to find the owner."

It was Adrian's backpack.

The women took Carlos to the mountain where they had found it. By then it was dark. Carlos had only a headlamp cutting through the night. He stood at the base of the mountain and called Adrian's name. The first time there was no response. The second time there was still nothing. The third time he heard something faint and broken.

Carlos followed the sound at the base of the mountain and found Adrian. Alive but severely injured and barely conscious.

Carlos did not ask him what happened or why. He looked at him and said, "It's not your time. I was sent to find you."

Carlos told me this on October 22, 2025, on the very day Adrian was flying to Costa Rica to return the jacket. The same jacket Carlos had left at my apartment in Logroño. The jacket I handed to Adrian the next morning to return to Carlos.

We sat in silence for a long moment, both of us crying, both of us understanding that we had not been meant to talk about music that morning. We had been meant to talk about this.

The Feeling I Ignored

When Carlos finally finished, I told him that when Adrian left my apartment, I felt something was off. I still do not know how to describe it. I only know that I felt it clearly and chose to ignore it because I did not understand what action it required. I have learned since then to trust those feelings, even when I cannot name them, even when the right action is not yet clear.

What frightened me most about Adrian's story was not that he jumped. It was that he stopped at a bar first. That moment before the decision, when one drink feels easier than silence. I recognized that immediately. I have been that man standing at the edge, choosing numbness over facing what I could not bear to feel.

I have been sober for more than four years now. Every morning I wake up and say the same thing: just for today, I will not drink, smoke, use Xanax or poppers. Not tomorrow. Not next week. Just today.

A few days after Adrian returned the jacket to Carlos in Costa Rica, I walked into an AA meeting in Miami. It was the first time I picked up a medallion. I met a man named Mario there. He told me he was celebrating thirty-four years of sobriety. I told him I was celebrating four. He smiled and offered to present my medallion, and I accepted.

When he placed it in my hand, I felt something settle. Four years. One thousand four hundred sixty days, lived one at a time. That is also *más allá*. Not only saving yourself, but allowing others to help you, and eventually helping someone else.

The Chain

I had believed the second Camino was about my healing, my search for home, my effort to stop chasing and start trusting. It was partly that. But it was also about Adrian, and Carlos, and a jacket left on a chair at a pilgrims' dinner. It was about opening my home and showing up without knowing what it might lead to.

I did not save Adrian. Carlos did. But I was part of the chain. The Camino does not end in Santiago. It continues through the lives it touches and the ways we carry it forward.

That is what *más allá* means. Beyond your own story. Beyond your own healing.

Sometimes you do not understand your part until much later. Sometimes you learn it during a call about business. Sometimes the man who tried to die is flying to return a jacket, and you finally see the shape of what you were walking toward all along.

I often think about that morning in Logroño. Adrian standing in the doorway. The feeling I did not trust. The ordinary moment that turned out to matter more than I could have known.

The Camino keeps reminding me what counts. Not the deal. Not the proof. Not the validation. But the meal, the extra room, the jacket, and the willingness to show up.

If this book reaches even one person, if it helps someone take a first step, make a call, walk into a meeting, to see themselves in a different light, or choose to keep going one more day, then everything I walked through was worth it.

Just for Today

This morning I woke up in Miami. I made coffee. I opened my journal and wrote what I write every day: Just for today, I will not drink, smoke, use Xanax or poppers. I told myself I love you, Michael and Mike, and I asked for God's grace to keep moving forward.

Adrian is alive in Costa Rica. Carlos has his jacket back. I am still walking.

I used to believe that arrival meant answers, that if I walked far enough or healed enough or succeeded enough, certainty would follow. What I understand now is simpler. I do not need certainty to be at peace. I do not need the future to cooperate for my life to be enough. I know who I am, and I trust how I move through the world.

The Camino did not give me a destination. It gave me myself.

So I move onward and forward, not because I am chasing anything, but because I am finally at home in my own skin, one step, one breath, one day at a time, in the grace of God.

That is all any of us ever has.

And it is enough.

Just for today.

La Vida es Más Allá — Life Is Beyond

THE END

PHOTOS FROM BOTH CAMINOS

Camino Francés 2022

Camino Francés & Camino Portugués 2025

Leaving Pamplona on my first full day on the Camino, September, 2022

Alto de Perdón September 2022

Somewhere in La Rioja, Spain September 2022

Starting in the early morning somewhere along the Meseta,
Spain September 2022

The path continues along the Meseta, Spain September 2022

Cruz de Ferro, Camino Francés 2022

At the base of O Cebreiro in the Galician Mountains, Spain

Riding up O Cebreiro Mountain, September 2022

At the top of O Cebreiro Mountain, Galicia, Spain 2022

Arriving in Santiago de Compostela, October 2022

Leaving Saint-Jean-Pied-de-Port, France August 2025

Heading into Roncesvalles, Spain August 2025

Leaving Porto, Portugal on the Camino Portugués, September 2025

Walking along the Portuguese coastline, September 2025

Sunset in Vigo, Spain September 2025

Outside of Vigo, Spain, September 2025

Walking under a canopy of grapes on the Camino Portugués, October 2025

The Santiago de Compostela Cathedral, Praza do Obradoiro

GRATITUDE

A heartfelt thank-you to Bryant, Lee, Kelly, Frankie, Stephen, Bill, Steven, David, Michel, John, Ray, Ted, Randy, Ana, Jill, Steve, and Cathy who have given me their love, time, and support over the years. To Dr. Bob, because I couldn't have imagined any of this without his years of work. To Seamus, Kevin, Leslie, Andrew, Neill, Merel, Marcus, Margie, Lisa, Toby, Ji, Marcel, Eric, Li, Donna, Paige, Lynn, and Bob S. for making my camino journeys that much richer. And finally to my grandmother, Buster, Steve, Freddy, Don and Buc: Save me a place at the table.

With deep gratitude to Holly Welker, who treated this book and the life behind it with extraordinary care, patience, and respect, and to Nuno Moreira, who listened deeply and gave the story a visual home worthy of the journey.

AUTHOR'S NOTE

If You're Ready to Walk Your Own Camino

When I finished writing this book, I realized something important: I'd spent these pages describing a transformation, but I hadn't told you what I do now with what I learned.

Since my second Camino in 2025, I've dedicated myself to coaching others through this journey. I guide select Camino experiences throughout the year—not as a tour operator who books your hotels and moves your bags (though logistics matter and I work with excellent partners for that), but as someone who walks alongside you through the internal journey that happens while you're crossing Spain.

I work with people in midlife who recognize they're living in warrior mode and are ready to discover what lies *más allá*—what lies beyond. People who've spent decades achieving, surviving, proving, and controlling, and who sense there's another way to live but don't quite know how to get there.

There are many ways to walk the Camino. You can plan it yourself with guidebooks and determination. You can hire a company to handle logistics and walk with strangers. You can join a large tour group and have the experience curated for you. All of these are valid.

But if this book resonated with you—if you saw yourself in these pages, if you recognized your own warrior mode and longed for something beyond it—then maybe we're meant to walk together.

I work with people who are genuinely ready to change, not just ready to take a nice trip to Spain. I work with people who understand that transformation requires honesty, vulnerability, and the willingness to look at the parts of themselves they've been running from.

If that's you, I'd be honored to guide or coach you.

Learn more about Camino Más Allá at:
www.caminomasalla.com
or email me directly at:
michael@caminomasalla.com

The Camino is waiting.

Más allá,
Michael

AUTHOR BIO

Michael Rucker is a Camino coach and guide who spent the first six decades of his life in warrior mode before the Camino de Santiago taught him there was another way to live.

Before coaching transformational Camino journeys, Michael spent over thirty years in music industry marketing and brand strategy, including more than a decade revitalizing the legendary Fania Records. He's worked with major entertainment brands, built successful consultancies, and learned the hard way that professional achievement doesn't cure spiritual emptiness.

At sixty, newly sober and uncertain about everything except that his old life wasn't working anymore, Michael walked the Camino Francés for the first time. At sixty-three, after slipping back into old patterns, he walked parts of both the Camino Francés and the Portuguese coastal route. He finally understood what transformation actually requires: not a single moment of revelation, but a daily practice of remembering what matters.

Michael guides select Camino experiences throughout the year through his company, Camino Más Allá, working with small groups and individuals seeking genuine transformation. He is fluent in Spanish, having lived extensively in Mexico City and Madrid. He holds a degree in marketing and has been an exchange student, foster kid, closeted corporate executive, and, finally, a man willing to tell the truth about his journey. He has over four years of continuous sobriety and maintains a daily practice that includes AA meetings, journaling, and his personal mantra: "Just for today I will not drink, smoke, use Xanax or poppers with you. I love you Michael and Mike. And I move onward and forward in the grace of God." He's still walking.

Under a Canopy of Grapes is his first book. He can be reached at:

michael@caminomasalla.com.

Michael's Playlist:

Spotify Public Playlist at marucker "Zipolite Volumen I".

www.ingramcontent.com/pod-product-compliance
Lightning Source LLC
LaVergne TN
LVHW090515110826
845146LV00003B/863

* 9 7 9 8 9 9 4 9 3 5 9 0 3 *